THE KINGDOM, THE SEED, & THE SOIL

DR. DON D. HUGHES

THE KINGDOM, THE SEED, & THE SOIL

CONTENTS

SECTION TWO

edition, version 13.0.0., copyright © 2000-2021, Rick Meyers. All Rights
Reserved Worldwide.

All references noted as Adam Clarke's Commentary are taken from Clarke, A.
(1869). Clarke's Commentary: The Holy Bible, containing the Old and New
Testaments: The Text printed from the most correct copies of the Present
Authorized Translation, including the marginal readings and parallel texts, with a
Commentary and Critical Notes.

The excerpts from Albert Barnes' Notes on the Bible, originally published
between 1847-85, are used in this work in accordance with the public domain
status of the text. These excerpts are sourced from e-Sword, and no copyright
restrictions apply to them. They are reproduced here for educational and
informational purposes.

All dictionary word definitions contained within this work are sourced from
Webster's Online Dictionary.

Cover design and graphics: David Munoz Art (davidmunoz.com)

Copyediting and format: L3 Editorial Consulting.

Also, as the author I choose to intentionally use the lowercase "s" when penning
satan's name.

Published by Rev House School of Ministry, Tulsa, Oklahoma. www.rhsom.com

All rights reserved.

INTRODUCTION

Never in my 49 years of ministry (at the release of my newest manuscript, February 2024, have I felt such an unction to release this timely and much needed Word into the Ekklesia (the Body of Christ). For almost five decades now I have ministered, taught, trained, challenged, and to the best of my ability, equipped the Church to walk in victory, overcome their challenges, to grow up IN HIM in all things, and ultimately to find, walk in, and fulfill their purpose and destiny.

In early fall 2023, I began a journey through the gospels, studying, researching and exegeting the Kingdom Parable of the Sower, which is found in Matthew, Mark, Luke, and the extra (as some would state) canonical Gospel of Thomas. And as usual, in the Holy Spirit's working/dealing with me over the years in my study time, He began to open these truths to me, to bring to light and unveil the truths revealed in this book. I can take no credit for the revelation you are about to embark on, as I am still His student and He is still the teacher.

In God's perfect timing, and I sincerely believe, "for such a time as this," the truths in this book and the answers made known to me and now being penned, will change the course of many lives within the church, individually and corporately. The growth, increase, and fruit that so many have desired and longed for, yet has seemed to evade (escape) them, will become a thing of the past. These truths will release the 100-60-30-fold fruit that the parable has promised.

Minds clouded with religious, man-made doctrines, wrong teachings, and fallacies (mistaken belief systems, especially those based on unsound, and the unfounded opinions of religion) will be exposed to the point that deliverance will/has come, fruit will be seen, peace will be restored to the hearts and minds of many. Condemnation is over!!! The truth is/will set you free.

In closing, my prayer for you is clearly this, "that the eyes of your understanding will be enlightened to the point that you may know (become intimate with) your calling, inheritance, and purpose as sons of God" (Ephesians 1:18). Prepare your heart and mind for the pages you are about to delve into, your life is going to be challenged, changed, and blessed.

His servant,
Dr. Don D Hughes

FOREWORD

From the Seeker.

Who I am does not necessarily matter, but what I am does. I started this journey of seeking more than fifty years ago and in that time, I have read more books than I can count. I read every day. I only seek for one thing, truth! The truth we hear/see and understand sets us free.

> John 8:31-32 Then said Jesus to those Jews which believed on him, If ye continue in my word, *then* are ye my disciples indeed; 32 And ye shall know the truth, and the truth shall make you free.

Truth is powerful.

Hebrews 4:12 For the word of God *is* quick, and powerful, and sharper than any two-edged sword, piercing even to the dividing asunder of soul and spirit, and of the joints and marrow, and *is* a discerner of the thoughts and intents of the heart.

I do not seek validation for what I already believe, I seek God's unchanging truth that will change me. I am not interested in information with no application. I said all of that to get to this one point. Outside of reading the Bible itself, this is the best book that I have ever read. I am stronger, happier, and freer than I have ever been.

Dr. Don Hughes, Thank you, my friend!

Your many weeks and months of prayer and hard work have helped me, and I honestly believe that anyone who reads this great book will also be helped.

Pastor Travis Bussey
Lighthouse Church
Thorsby, Alabama

ENDORSEMENTS

I have known Apostle Don Hughes for ten-plus years now, and not only is he one my best friends in ministry, but he is also one of the best and most thorough teachers of God's word that I know. His solid exegesis of the Scriptures is once again on full display in this latest literary work that he has been inspired to pen.

In *The Kingdom, The Seed, & The Soil* you will be challenged to realize and know what Jesus intended for all his disciples to know. Even as the disciples questioned him: *"Why do you speak to the people in parables?"* Jesus replied: *"The knowledge of the secrets of heaven has been given to you, but it has not been given to them."* **Matthew 13:10-11**. (The Voice Translation)

Take an inside look into the master parable that Jesus taught, because understanding this one will unlock the meaning of all the parables. It is with all confidence that I fully endorse this manuscript from my "brother from another mother."

Apostle Michael Fram
Prophetic Destiny Ministries International
Sayreville, NJ USA

I first met Dr. Don Hughes in 1976 while we were attending Rhema Bible School in Broken Arrow, Oklahoma. I have known him for quite some time and am honored not only to call him my friend, but a true covenant brother. He has always opened up the scriptures in such a revealing way, helping us to see and understand them.

Once again, he certainly has not disappointed us in his newest book, *The Kingdom, The Seed, & The Soil*. The truths revealed in this book will cause you to bloom where God plants you, you will produce a harvest that will bring him much glory.

Your destiny, calling, abundance, everything that you need is ALREADY in you in seed form. Our life (our soil) determines how our seed will germinate through the teaching in this book. I am very happy to endorse this new book by Dr. Don Hughes.

Ron Kidman
(Minister, Mentor)
Jackson, Michigan

I am so honored to endorse this new manuscript; I believe that it is one of the best books you will ever read for those who are truly in pursuit of our Lord. Apostle Don Hughes is a son to our Heavenly Father, a father to many, and one who has faithfully pursued God for many years. He has experienced many battles and has operated in many areas of ministry and has functioned in each one of the ascension gifts.

He has remained faithful to the cause of Christ in the earth, and every year that I have known him, I have experienced change in his life from glory to glory. He has become one of God's generals in our day, as an apostle of God teaching us the word and breaking it down where we are able to hear, understand, and live until there is great fruit.

This book is definitely a grand slam of his many years of experience and from the transformation that has taken place in his life. I have heard and read many messages regarding the power of the seed but never from a kingdom perspective. This book will help you not only to have revelation, but also a change of heart that will cause one to fully follow our Lord. This book will help many come out of religious mindsets that have been fruitless and have not produced a harvest. This book, *The Kingdom, The Seed & The Soil* will remove wrong thinking and cultivate hearts so that the message of the Kingdom can begin to change you from the inside out.

Thanks, my friend and co-laborer, as a senior council member of Love & Unity and a true apostle and writer of our time. You are a blessing, and I believe this book will change many lives and bring many into maturity. We are wanting and desiring for more than just words, but a true manifestation of the mature sons of God. This teaching will help us get another step closer to the advancement of His Kingdom in all the world.

Apostle Eddie Maestas
Founder/Visionary
Love & Unity Movement
Pomona, CA

Over the past four years (as of 2024), Apostle Don Hughes has been a teacher, a mentor, a spiritual father, and a friend to me. I know him to be a man of honor and integrity, who is a conscientious steward of God's Word. He carefully and deliberately examines the Word of God by the leading of the Holy Spirit, attentively exegeting every scripture for knowledge, truth, and understanding that is applied for wisdom.

He has remained true to his pattern in this latest examination of the Parable of the Sower. Prepare to see the parable Jesus taught in an entirely new way. Expect to receive powerful revelation concerning the condition of the soil (heart, mind) and which type of soil every believer should be cultivating.

The Kingdom, The Seed, & The Soil is a valuable book for your journey into the Kingdom. You will have a greater understanding about your responsibility to be the "good soil" that God intended. You will propagate the seed He planted inside of you and manifest according to His design and purpose to yield "good fruit." I recommend this book by Dr. Don Hughes to every believer who desires growth and freedom from mediocrity.

Geneva Hollis
Spiritual Daughter
Calera, Alabama

CHAPTER ONE

WHY DID JESUS SPEAK IN PARABLES?

SOME REFERENCES QUOTE JESUS AS TEACHING MORE THAN 50 parables throughout the gospels (Matthew, Mark, Luke, John). Have you ever wondered as to why so much of Jesus's speaking to the multitudes, religious leaders and even His disciples were in parables?

First, let us define what a parable is from the Greek language. It is the Greek word, "*parabole*" (pronounced: par-ab-ol-ay). It translates as, "the comparison of one thing with another, a likeness, a similitude, an example by which either the duties of men or the things of God, particularly, the nature and history of God's kingdom are figuratively portrayed." Simply put, "a parable is an **earthly story** with a **heavenly meaning**." (Also check out my book, *The Kingdom of Heaven is Like*, available on Amazon or through my ministry.)

Some History

IN **MATTHEW 3:16-17**, JESUS IS BAPTIZED BY JOHN THE BAPTIST in the Jordan river, the heavens open and God acknowledges and declares Him as His son. Jesus goes into the wilderness temptation and comes out victorious over every test that the enemy presented Him with. In **Matthew 4:17**, He establishes His purpose and message, to challenge the mindsets of the religious systems/structures of His day by preaching the message of the kingdom.

Matthew 3:16-17

16 When John had administered the rite of baptism with Jesus in the Jordan, he sprung up out of the river, (the Greek speaks of "any kind of separation of one thing from another by which the union or fellowship of the two is destroyed.") The death, burial, resurrection and baptism of Jesus separated life from death, Christ from Adam, light from darkness, the law from grace, and the heavens that had been shut up because of Satan, Adam, sin, and death were once again open because the cause and the culprit had been defeated, the dove that had been circling since Noah could finally land again. (DHP)

17 Now, once again, the father God breaks the silence with this resounding revelation, he is my esteemed, dear beloved son, completely resembling me once again like my created son Adam did before his fall. I take great delight in him, I take great pleasure in him, I prefer him, I chose him, he is mine. Dr. Hughes paraphrase. (DHP)

Matthew 4:17

17 From that time forward, Jesus started to proclaim with gravity (extreme importance, with all seriousness) and authority requiring all to reconsider their past mindsets (patterns of thought) and to begin to think differently in order to see and understand his message, which was his mission and now being declared through him, heavens kingdom (pattern) was now being revealed in the earth. (DHP)

In **Verse 23**, He continues teaching the kingdom message in the synagogues (notice, He did not change His message. As a matter of fact, He preached the same message for 3.5 years) and look at the evidence, the manifestations that happened as He preached the kingdom. Sickness and disease healed, demon-possessed delivered, lunatic (epileptic) and palsy (paralytic, disabled) also healed. Maybe we are not getting the results and manifestations Jesus did because we are preaching everything but what Jesus preached. Many preach messages about Jesus, but have never preached the message Jesus preached, The Kingdom. The right message brings the right manifestations. You need more proof? In **Matthew 24:14**, Jesus stated,

"And the gospel of the kingdom shall be preached in all the world for a witness unto all nations; and then shall the end come." **Matthew 24:14**

What if the wrong messages being preached is the very thing holding back his **appearing**? Selah!

14 This gospel (glad tiding) of God's kingdom, dominion, rule, and reign proclaimed, and published, it must be heard and obeyed. It must be made known to the entire world (all the inhabited earth), there will be evidence, proof, even testimonies throughout all tribes, nations, and people groups, at that time, the aim and purpose of this message will be fulfilled. (DHP)

At the end of His earthly ministry, after His resurrection, He appeared during a forty-day period, over and over to individuals by infallible (undeniable, indubitable, impossible to doubt) proofs. I am led to believe that during those final forty days on earth before His ascension, the last things He would say would be of the utmost importance to the hearer. Again, even after His resurrection, He still did not deviate from what He began coming out of the wilderness. **Acts 1:3**, *"being seen of them forty days and speaking of the things pertaining to the kingdom of God."* In my best lawyer language, "I rest my case." His message never changed!

Acts 1:3

3 For forty days following his exit from death, hell and the grave, his passion to fulfill his mission (purpose) along with God's unequaled power/authority raised him from death to life, from the grave and eventually back to the garden. His continual appearing during those forty days, he was seen by many with such indubitable, unquestionable evidence that there was no denying he had risen. During his final forty days, he continued to speak, teach, exhort, and affirm his kingdom assignment, purpose, and message. (DHP)

So herein lies the question to consider, why did Jesus so often speak in parables to the multitudes?

A Provoking Thought from Dr. Myles Munroe

I was watching a video message from Dr. Myles Munroe on YouTube sometime back and he made a statement that caught my attention to the point that I stopped the video and thought about his comment. He said, *"God doesn't automatically volunteer information (revelation)."*[1] As I considered his words, immediately some scriptures came to mind. In Matthew's gospel, Jesus spoke about asking, seeking, and knocking and then revealed those who "ask receive, those who seek find, and those who knock, the door will open."

Matthew 7:7-8

7 Ask, crave, and desire, then it will be granted, furnished, supplied, given to the one asking, seek in order to find (by thinking, meditating, enquiring into), pursue, and after searching, what you sought after will come upon you, it will be found, detected, recognized and discovered, and finally, knock at the door (of the kingdom) and it will open and what is on the other side of the door will be revealed. (DHP)

8 Everyone individually and collectively that craves and desires, they will lay hold and obtain it, those who seek with the intention of finding, what they seek will come into their possession, and finally, the door of the kingdom (and its understanding) will be opened to that knock. (DHP)

There are other scriptures and references to the individual having a part to play in receiving their answer, their need met, even their miracle. Jesus asks the man with the thirty-eight-year infirmity at the pool of Bethesda what he wanted, *"Do you want to be made whole?"* Jesus gave very direct commands to him after he made his excuses, *"Rise, pick up your bed and walk."* The man had to respond, he had to act on Jesus words, when he did his part, Jesus did his part. (**John 5:1-9**)

In **2 Kings**, Naaman, the captain of the host of the king of Syria was a great man, but he was a leper. He heard of a prophet in Samaria that could recover him from leprosy. Naaman shows up at the house of Elisha and here comes the test, the prophet did not even speak to him but sent his messenger, again, with a very specific word, *"Go and wash in the Jordan seven times and your flesh will become clean and new."* Then after he had worked through his own pride, arrogance and anger, in obedience to the prophet's messenger and his own servant, he went and submerged himself seven times in the river, and just as it had been proclaimed, he became leprosy free. (Naaman had to do some asking, seeking, and knocking to get his answer and his miracle) **2 Kings 5:1-14**.

In **Mark 10**, Blind Bartimaeus heard about Jesus, then searched as to where he would be, positioned himself as to the place Jesus would pass, and his knocking took on the form of words. *"Jesus, thou Son of David, have mercy on me. And Jesus stood still."* His pursuit of Jesus caused him to stop moving and stand still, then he asks Bartimaeus what he wanted. After hearing, He gave him instruction. When he heard the request, Bartimaeus acted, and Jesus responded in like fashion (**Mark 10:46-52**).

———

LET ME GIVE A COUPLE MORE EXAMPLES FOR CLARIFICATION AND confirmation. Jesus was teaching a parable in **Luke 18** on the "Unjust Judge." There was a widow woman that continued to trouble (pursue) this judge to avenge her of her enemy (adversary). Jesus said that she did this continually to the point of wearying the judge. Again, notice she was pursuing, asking, seeking, and knocking until the judge acted. He then declares that Go, who is just and faithful will vindicate, bring retribution to those who pursue, who implore Him day and night. He then asks an interesting question, when He appears, will He find the same level of faith and commitment from His own? Selah! (**Luke 18:1-8**).

Proverbs 8:17

I have great affection for those who love (have great affection) me, those who earnestly search, enquire, seek diligently, especially early in approaching/doing any task, I will appear, and they will attain (succeed in achieving) what they have pursued. (DHP)

Hebrews 11:6

Apart from faith, without true conviction that God IS (creator, ruler, provider and faithful), you become impotent, without strength, disabled, all which gives him no pleasure, when you come near to approach God, of necessity (it is only right and proper, it is required). You must have conviction, confidence in and complete trust because of and concerning all that he is, then he appears, comes upon the stage in your life and restores, rewards, and remunerates (pays wages, spiritually and naturally). He gives back to you by reason of your seeking him out, your diligent and earnest pursuit of him, you're craving for him will find him and all that He is and possesses. (DHP)

I believe as we progress further into this manuscript, the Parable of the Sower taught by Jesus, which is the theme and the reason this book was written, will continue to shed light and illumination into the above concept. It will become even clearer in our understanding.

> Author's Note: THIS BOOK WAS FIRST TAUGHT AT LENGTH, IN DETAIL TO OUR CONGREGATION, REV HOUSE FELLOWSHIP, IN BROKEN ARROW, OKLAHOMA, THEN PROMPTED BY THE HOLY SPIRIT AND CONFIRMED BY OTHERS, I SAT DOWN, RESTUDIED IT AND THEN WROTE THIS BOOK YOU NOW HOLD IN YOUR HAND.

I am convinced, with a heavy mandate to release, that the truths published herein will pull back the curtain, will unclutter the minds, will turn on the light, and ultimately set those at liberty who have been captive by all appearances to seemingly fruitless or at best limited fruit in their lives, ministries, marriages, businesses, and life's endeavors.

James writes and reminds us of the importance of patience while the fruit is growing, developing, and maturing.

James 5:7

Be patient therefore, brethren, unto the coming of the Lord. Behold, the husbandman waiteth for the precious fruit of the earth, and hath long patience for it, until he receive the early and latter rain.

***

My brothers, my fellow believers, born from the same womb, do not lose heart, persevere, be brave. The presence and appearing of the Lord are guaranteed (He has appeared, is appearing, and will appear), the tiller of the soil (that is us) expects, waits, and looks for the fruit, as he knows the great price the seed pays to bring about growth, maturity and finally the harvest. The earth coupled with the rain are key factors in the seed's potential. The final manifestation comes after two specific seasons of rain once the seed has been sown and cultivated, the early (fall) rain and the latter (spring) rain. The early rain develops the seed, the latter matures the seed. (DHP)

---

1. Finding The Kingdom Of God Part 1: Essential Teachings By Dr. Myles Munroe | MunroeGlobal.com | https://youtu.be/GrzeDNU8rds?si=oIr065JBMQJEAK5O

YOUR PURSUIT & SOIL DETERMINES (DICTATES) THE FRUIT

WHILE I WAS STUDYING THIS SUBJECT, AND BEGAN TO TEACH IT IN OUR HOME CHURCH, REV HOUSE FELLOWSHIP, DURING THE THIRD SUNDAY OF THIS SERIES, AT THE END OF THE SERVICE, ONE OF MY DAUGHTERS IN THE FAITH, PROPHET ANITA DUANE RAISED HER HAND AND SAID, *"POP, YOUR PURSUIT DETERMINES YOUR FRUIT."* THANKS HON.

THUS THE TITLE OF CHAPTER TWO WITH A COUPLE KEY WORDS ADDED.

I DO WANT TO CONTINUE THE THOUGHTS FROM CHAPTER ONE AND expound on them a little further, as I believe this insight is vitally important to understanding the Kingdom Parable we are about to unveil.

There is a concept in the New Testament that must be examined as we move forward. Jesus never had a problem gathering a multitude or getting a crowd for a myriad of reasons, either based on his reputation, the miracles he manifested, and at times the "free lunch" program (this will be brought to light further in this chapter). It brings up an honest question. Why were they following Him? Why are we following Him?

Perform a few miracles, get your name out there, raise the dead, cast out some devils, and His reputation would produce crowds, multitudes (See **John 6:2**), which one day produced a crowd of 5000 men (plus women and children, they did not count them back then). There was only one little boy's lunch. Jesus took it, blessed it, and again, performed another miracle. The "free lunch program" started (kind of like today's coffee and donut churches), and Jesus's statement in **John 6:26** exposed the heart/soil of them (read **Verses 22-26**).

26 Jesus answered them and said, Verily, verily, I say unto you, Ye seek me, not because ye saw the miracles, but because ye did eat of the loaves, and were filled.

> 26 Jesus answered their question and said firmly and truthfully (double emphasizing, verily, verily), "you did not search for me, seek me out just because you beheld the miracles, signs, and wonders, authenticating that I am sent from God, you searched for me because you consumed (devoured) the bread that I had blessed, and your desire was satisfied. (DHP)

The Multitudes, The Seventy, The Twelve, The Three, and The One

MIRACLES, REPUTATION, AND FOOD PRODUCED THE MULTITUDES, and initially seventy other disciples plus the twelve, they all were pursuing, as to what/why, well that is being explained in these first two chapters. If you continue reading all of **John 6**, some insightful things are seen. After expressing His thoughts as to why they were following Him (**Verse 26** above), the challenge/separation comes to those who were following and why. In **Verses 53-58**, He begins the discourse, the challenge to their pursuit.

I believe He was revealing "**Covenant 101**" to them, the free lunch program was over, their pursuit and what they were pursuing was going to be taken to the next level, or at least uncovered. He was not speaking of cannibalism, He was referencing covenant. From then on, they had to pursue **Him,** not what He gave them. He was offering them the God life, His nature, power, and all God-given power and ability.

Their response in **Verse 60** showed where they were. *"This is a hard saying; who can hear it?"*

> This decree is offensive, harsh, stern, and too severe, who can really accept and obey it (DHP)?

The disciples murmured, grumbled (Greek-conferred secretly together) and complained, then comes the separation because of the requirement of His pursuit. Notice **Verse 66**:

After his comments, many (the seventy) of his students, pupils and disciples departed, went back (no longer moving forward and pursuing), disappeared, and stopped following, they progressed no further, they just walked away. (DHP)

Jesus then turns to the twelve remaining disciples after the dust had settled from the mass exodus and asks, *"Will ye also go away?"* (KJV). In exegeting the context from the Greek, the language is much stronger as Jesus looks at them and voices strongly, *"You can go too if you want to! Then Peter responds with, "Lord, where are we going to go now? you are the Word of God, revealed, alive and living."*

———

JESUS NEVER PLAYED FAVORITES, HE LIVED BY PRINCIPLES AND responded often to man's pursuit. Those (His disciples) who pursued Him the most got the closest to Him. There was always the twelve, often Peter, James, and John went and were taken further. And finally you have John the Beloved, the Revelator (the one who loved Jesus, always hanging on to Him, probably teased some by the other apostles, however he wrote the last book of the canon of the scriptures, Revelation, which is the unveiling of Jesus Christ. See **Revelation 1:1**, *"The Revelation of Jesus Christ…"*

A final thought. It is quite interesting after Jesus speaks of covenant with the seventy and the twelve, and talks about their pursuit and the cost. Then, after their hearts/soil is revealed, they leave. Have you ever noticed, this is recorded in John 666 (left colon out on purpose)? Selah!

Pursuit

Pursuit defines simply as, "the action of following or pursuing someone or something." Some synonyms are, "chasing, shadowing, seeking, **going all out**, inquiring, hunting."

In Matthew's gospel, Jesus approaches four men whose occupation was fishermen. They were the ones experienced in "throwing the nets," and here comes the Lord and what does He do? He cast a spiritual net (calling) in their direction, then waited for their response. What they did, how they responded would today be, at best, very uncommon. They left "their nets" and picked up His! No debate, no fasting, and praying for days on end, not needing confirmation. They followed.

Matthew 4:18-22

18 And Jesus, walking by the sea of Galilee, saw two brethren, Simon called Peter, and Andrew his brother, **casting a net** into the sea: for they were fishers.

19 And he saith unto them, **Follow me, and I will make you fishers of men**.

20 And they straightway **left *their* nets**, and followed him.

21 And going on from thence, he saw other two brethren, James *the son* of Zebedee, and John his brother, in a ship with Zebedee their father, **mending their nets**; and he called them.

22 And they immediately left the ship and their father, and followed him.

***

18 Jesus, the Son of God was passing by the sea of Galilee and gave his attention to two men, Simon Peter and his brother Andrew, they were throwing their nets into the sea, this was their livelihood. (DHP)

19 Jesus then spoke to them and said, "come here, walk with me, and I will prepare you for your ultimate purpose, calling, and destiny, the nets you will now throw will gather in humanity, men and women. (DHP)

20 Then, immediately, at once, they put away their nets, by their actions, said yes to the Lord and accompanied him (the Greek also states to become a disciple). (DHP)

21 As they left there, he perceived two more men, James, Zebedee's son, and his brother John, they were in a ship with their father repairing and putting their nets in order, he bid them just as he had Peter and Andrew. (DHP)

22 Immediately upon receiving Jesus commission, James and John left their ship, nets, even their father and accompanied him (soon to become disciples also). (DHP)

Your Pursuit Will Cost You (*and Reveal Where You Are*)

MATTHEW 19:16-25

16 And, behold, one came and said unto him, Good Master, what good thing shall I do, that I may have eternal life?

17 And he said unto him, Why callest thou me good? *there is* none good but one, *that is,* God: but if thou wilt enter into life,

15

keep the commandments.

18 He saith unto him, Which? Jesus said, Thou shalt do no murder, Thou shalt not commit adultery, Thou shalt not steal, Thou shalt not bear false witness,

19 Honour thy father and *thy* mother: and, Thou shalt love thy neighbour as thyself.

20 The young man saith unto him, All these things have I kept from my youth up: what lack I yet?

21 Jesus said unto him, If thou wilt be perfect, go *and* sell that thou hast, and give to the poor, and thou shalt have treasure in heaven: and come *and* follow me.

22 But when the young man heard that saying, he went away sorrowful: for he had great possessions.

23 Then said Jesus unto his disciples, Verily I say unto you, That a rich man shall hardly enter into the kingdom of heaven.

24 And again I say unto you, It is easier for a camel to go through the eye of a needle, than for a rich man to enter into the kingdom of God.

25 When his disciples heard *it,* they were exceedingly amazed, saying, who then can be saved?

In essence, this rich young ruler was questioning Jesus as to what it was going to take, what was it going to cost him to pursue Him, to receive what He was offering—eternal life. I tend to think Jesus's first response to the man's question was entry-level, to reel him in so to speak. Jesus wanted to reveal the heart/soil condition that for all intents and purposes would hinder the ruler's request.

Jesus said, *"Just keep the commandments, don't commit adultery, don't shed innocent blood, don't steal, don't be an untrue testifier (don't offer what is false as true), honor your parents, and finally, love (agape) your fellowman, care for and be concerned for them as you are yourself."*

Can you imagine the sigh of relief? *"Well Master, I have done all this since I was very young, am I still falling short in something, is there something that will take me out of the race and potentially hinder me from reaching the goal?"*

At this point Jesus deals with the heart issue, with the man's soil:

Matthew 19:21-22

21 Jesus makes known the cost of pursuit, immediately exposing the real heart issue, if you truly intend to and are determined to become a fully grown adult (spiritually), sell that which you possess, then give, supply, help, furnish those which are destitute, afflicted, and powerless to accomplish something for themselves, at that point, I will release into your possession what's now in my possession, my storehouse (treasury) will be at available to you, heaven's resources will be yours. (DHP)

22 When the rich young ruler considered what Jesus had said to him, he departed, he went back (not forward), full of sadness, grieved (one definition from the Greek says, "offended"), distressed, all because he had acquired much, estates, properties, and fields. (DHP)

My personal belief is that **his possessions owned him, he did not own his possessions**. He did not understand the kingdom's principle of sowing and reaping, giving, and receiving, seed, time, and harvest. His action, going back, revealed his heart and soil. One other thought [mine]. I am not totally convinced Jesus would have **required him to sell all, but he had to be willing to**. Remember, what the Apostle Paul referenced writing to the Corinthian church (**1 Corinthians 13:3**), and teaching what we call the love chapter. He stated we could give all our goods (possessions, wealth, and properties) to the poor and still struggle operating in the agape of God (Selah)!

Matthew quoted Jesus in his writings and said:

Matthew 15:8

8 This people draweth nigh unto me with their mouth, and honoureth me with *their* lips; but **their heart is far from me**.

The Greek word for heart is "*kardia*" (pronounced: kar-dee-ah) and defines as, "denoting the center (seat) of all physical and spiritual life."

Jesus was stating there are certain people who say the right things (that can be heard and seen externally) yet the problem, the issue, the deception is internally, in the heart, the unseen realm, the soil if you will (my thoughts).

8 There are people (and groups) that approach me with their words (language), even speaking of honor and reverence, but their heart is the true revealer, the hidden internals (that man can't see but that I know), and there is a great difference, a great gulf (ravine, chasm) between their spoken words and what is hidden in their heart, the two don't line up. (DHP)

——————

HOSEA, ONE OF THE MINOR PROPHETS IN THE OLD TESTAMENT penned these words during a certain season with God's people, "they were destroyed (Hebrew- failed, perished, to become undone) because they rejected (Hebrew- abhorred, despised, disdained, loathed, refused) knowledge" (See **Hosea 4:6**). John's gospel unfolds again the concept of pursuit:

JOHN 8:31-32

31 Then said Jesus to those Jews which believed on him, If ye continue in my word, *then* are ye my disciples indeed;

32 And ye shall know the truth, and the truth shall make you free.

31 Jesus spoke to those of Jewish origin who had faith in him, "you become a student (pupil, learner, disciple) when you abide, remain, and live in my word (Greek- *"logos"*, the revealed, written sayings of God). (DHP)

32 When you come to know (a Jewish idiom of sexual intercourse between a man and a woman), when you become intimate with the sayings of God and the duties of men. That intimacy will receive the seed (the engrafted word) which will then reveal the seed, and the result will set you at liberty, free you from sin's dominion, it will change you from a slave to a son. (DHP)

Meditate on these first two chapters, pray over them, read them again, let the scales, the blinders be removed, so that the light of revelation can flood your heart. Change your soil because fruit is coming!

CHAPTER THREE

A SYNOPTIC LOOK AT THE GOSPELS OF THE PARABLE OF THE SOWER

A COMPARISON OF MATTHEW, MARK, LUKE, & THE GOSPEL ACCORDING TO THOMAS (SEE ARTICLES AND INFORMATION BELOW ON THE GOSPEL ACCORDING TO THOMAS).

SEE THE DEFINITION OF THE WORD **PARABLE** IN THE BEGINNING OF Chapter One. In a synopsis of the gospels, three of the four share the events and the teaching by Jesus of this parable. Much to my amazement and surprise, as I was researching the internet in writing this manuscript, I found an original copy (first printed in 1959) of *The Gospel According To Thomas*. No, it is not in the 66 books of what we refer to as the canon of scripture, yet there have been other manuscripts/writings found that were referenced, but were decided against being included.

I feel it necessary to share these two articles for some understanding and clarification, even though it is not necessarily the subject of this writing. The Bible is considered the inspired word of God by believers throughout the world. So, you have to wonder: where did it come from? With all the writings floating around the ancient world, who decided which of them rated as sacred enough to be scripture?

———

ARTICLE #1

This question is technically one of canonicity. **Canon** means norm or standard. The term was first applied by St. Athanasius to a collection of Jewish and Christian writings around the year 350. A fourth-century bishop of Alexandria, Egypt, Athanasius was a powerhouse.

He would later be named "Doctor of Orthodoxy" for his strong defense against heresies of his time. Athanasius attended the all-important Council of Nicaea, from which we get our Nicene Creed. He was a zealous advocate for the divinity of Jesus in an age before the nature of Jesus was uniformly accepted. For all of these reasons, Athanasius was invested in settling the canon of scripture: which books might be counted as the "Word of God"—and which, at best, were just good words.

It would have been helpful to him if the apostles had sat down one dull night in the first century and decided this themselves: *"Matthew, Mark, Luke, and John are in. Gospels of Thomas and Judas—out!"* It would also have been impossible since many New Testament texts were not written until after that first generation of church leaders had died. Also, strange as it may seem, even the Hebrew scriptures we call the Old Testament had yet to be defined by the Jewish community. While we may think of Jesus carrying around a volume of Genesis through Maccabees in his backpack, neither He nor anyone else of His time owned such a collection.

What hastened the need to settle the biblical canon was simple practicality. As the Christian community gradually separated from its Jewish roots, it was vital to determine which of the many instructive texts scattered around the Mediterranean region would be binding for each group. The rabbis of Judaism fought their own canon skirmishes around the year 100, but some books written before the time of Jesus that did not make their final list had already proven useful to Jewish Christians.

Heavy hitters among ancient theologians, such as Origen, Athanasius, and Jerome, argued for a shorter canon than Augustine, especially when it came to these Hebrew books. The 27 books Athanasius proposed for the New Testament were not much in dispute and remain standard today. It took the Council of Trent (1545-63) to define the Old Testament canon as inclusive of books that Protestant Reformers removed, including Tobit, Judith, Sirach, Wisdom, the Maccabees, and others. Today's Bible owes a debt to these many ancient debates.

This article appeared in the April 2012 issue of **U.S. Catholic** *(Vol. 77, No. 4, page 46).*

———

ARTICLE #2

The Old Testament books were written well before Jesus's Incarnation, and all of the New Testament books were written by roughly the end of the first century A.D. But the Bible as a whole was not officially compiled until the late fourth century, illustrating that it was the Catholic Church who determined the canon—or list of books—of the Bible under the guidance of the Holy Spirit. Indeed, the Bible is not a self-canonizing collection of books, as there is no table of contents included in any of the books.

Although the New Testament canon was not determined until the late 300s, books the Church deemed sacred were early on proclaimed at Mass, and read and preached about otherwise. Early Christian writings outnumbered the 27 books that would become the canon of the New Testament. The shepherds of the Church, by a process of spiritual discernment and investigation into the liturgical traditions of the Church spread throughout the world, had to draw clear lines of distinction between books that are truly inspired by God and originated in the apostolic period, and those which only claimed to have these qualities.

The process culminated in 382 as the Council of Rome, which was convened under the leadership of Pope Damasus I, promulgated the 73-book scriptural canon. The biblical canon was reaffirmed by the regional councils of Hippo (393) and Carthage (397), and then definitively reaffirmed by the ecumenical Council of Florence in 1442.

Finally, the ecumenical Council of Trent solemnly defined this same canon in 1546, after it came under attack by the first Protestant leaders, including Martin Luther (catholic.com/qa/who-compiled-the-bible-and-when).

These next few paragraphs explain when and where the Gospel of Thomas and other writings were found (from the inside cover of the book).

The remains of an extraordinary Coptic library, lost for 16 centuries and discovered in 1945 in a ruined tomb near Nag Hammadi, Upper Egypt, has yielded an extensive collection of *logia*, an anthology of 114 *Sayings of Jesus,* now published for the first time in their entirety. Preserved by dry sands covering what was apparently a thriving Gnostic community, 13 leather-bound papyrus volumes were found in jars in a cliffside by Egyptian peasants. Alone among the 49 works contained in them, *The Gospel of Thomas* has created a stir similar to that which followed the finding of the Dead Sea Scrolls, and has engaged the attention of the public at large as well as that of the learned world.

This document, containing many sayings never before seen, in addition to those resembling the New Testament and patristic texts, is an exceptional find. It is one of the earliest manuscripts related to the New Testament, and is based on fact, on "a work the primitive text of which must have been produced in Greek about AD 140."

In addition, there is a prologue attributing their recording and preservation to the apostle, Didymus Judas Thomas.

———

PRIMARILY, WE WILL BE USING MATTHEW'S ACCOUNT AS THE main text for the duration of this manuscript, however, we will examine the other gospels where it was recorded for further insight and revelation. The following are thoughts, quotes, and exegetes from certain words/phrases in the synopsis of the gospels on the subject of the Parable of the Sower.

HERE IS THE PARABLE AS RECORDED BY THOMAS:

The Gospel According to Thomas

Log 9 (page 7)

Whoever has ears to hear let him hear. **4** Jesus said: See, the sower went out, he filled his hand and, he threw. Some (seeds) fell on the road; **6** the birds came, they gathered them. **Others fell on the rock and did not strike root, 8 in the earth** and did not produce ears. And others fell on the thorns; **10** they choked the seed and the worm ate them. And others fell on the good earth; **12** and it brought forth good fruit; it bore sixty per measure and one hundred twenty per measure. (This is the exact wording as found in *The Gospel According to Thomas,* New York And Evanston, Harper & Row, Copyright, E. J. Brill, 1959).

The phrase in **Verse 7** caught my attention. The seed *"fell on the rock and did not strike root in the earth."* The primary root is called the "radicle," it is the first thing to emerge from the seed. This radicle anchors the plant to the ground (soil) and then it begins to absorb water. As the root absorbs the water, a shoot emerges from the seed planted.

The root that develops directly from the radicle is called the **"true root."** The root of the plant that develops from the radicle is the embryonic root which is located at the lower end of the embryonic axis or the primary root of the seed. The radicle is the first organ to emerge from the germinating seed and grows downwards into the soil, anchoring the seedling and absorbing water and nutrients from the soil. As the radicle grows and develops, it gives rise to lateral roots, which further expand the root system of the plant and facilitates the uptake of water and nutrients from the soil.(*This paragraph was written by a college graduate from Osmania University, graduated 2020, who majored in Botany Cytogenetics, Molecular Genetics & Biotechnology. Found on the Quora App*[1]).

As you can plainly see in the above stated paragraphs, the seed and the soil have very specific dynamics in order to work together for the desired result. Thomas stated that the rocky ground was the hindrance to the seed taking root. Again, the soil was the issue, not the seed. I believe that I am safe to say that the return, (fruit, harvest) is primarily based on the soil, not the seed.

———

LUKE'S ACCOUNT:

Luke penned his account of the parable in **Luke 8:4-15**, we will only investigate **Verse 15**. I believe that my paraphrase will further expand the phrase in bold below.

15 But that on the good ground are they, which **in an honest and good heart, having heard the word, keep *it*, and bring forth fruit with patience**.

15 The good ground (excellent in its nature and characteristics, genuine and approved for harvest, and fertile) are those who possess an honorable, excellent, upright, and distinguished heart

(the center and seat of all physical and spiritual life), they give audience and attention to what is being taught and announced, the logos (written-revealed) sayings, decrees, mandates, and sayings of God and His Kingdom, they don't just hear, they hold fast, they take firm possession of what they heard, and because their soil (heart) is fertile, they are fruitful and patient even in the fruits development and process, remaining steadfast, consistent, even cheerfully enduring knowing it is coming. (DHP)

Matthew's Account:

Matthew wrote concerning this parable in **Matthew 13:1-23**. We will examine **Verses 5-6**.

5 Some fell upon stony places, where they had not much earth: and forthwith they sprung up, because they had no deepness of earth:

> **5** Part of the seed descended upon rocky surfaces, in this place, there were more rocks than soil (earth which is necessary), at once, almost immediately a shoot appeared above the ground, but the fruits potential was denied as there was no depth (abundance) of the proper soil. (DHP)

The Preachers Homiletical Commentary says, "not soil containing loose stones, but a bed of rock, with only a slight covering of soil."[2]

6 And when the sun was up, they were scorched; and because they had no root, they withered away.

6 Then, when the heat escalated because the rays of the sun increased, the torture (the trial, persecution, and tribulation) from the heat burned up what had sprung up, there was no depth of root as a result of no depth of soil, it's potential harvest dried up as the consequence of the shallowness of the soil and the absence of moisture (water). (DHP)

Mark's Account:

Mark wrote his account of this in **Mark 4:1-20**, We will examine **Verses 2, 5, 7, 8, 13, and 15**.

2 And he taught them many things by parables, and said unto them in his **doctrine**,

2 He imparted instruction (expounded doctrine) often (frequently) in parables revealing the duties of men and the things of God, many times dealing with the nature and history of God's kingdom. He would tell earthly stories that carried heavenly meanings. (DHP)

5 And some fell on stony ground, where it had not much earth; and immediately it **sprang up, because it had no depth of earth**:

5 Other seed fell on ground dominated by rocks (the hindrance to growth and lasting fruit) with little or no soil (earth), almost immediately, you could see the beginning of a shoot coming up out of the rocky ground, the rock hindered the seed from reaching a depth in the soil (earth), to develop a deep a strong root system to sustain the seed during germination, development, growth and eventually harvest. (DHP)

7 And some fell among thorns, and the thorns grew up, and **choked it, and it yielded no fruit**.

> 7 Some seed the Sower released landed in thorny plants, briar bushes (woody thorns, prickly stems), as the thorns continued to grow, to spring up, in the end, they completely strangled the seed sown to the point that the seed yielded no benefit, advantage, profit or fruit. (DHP)

8 And other fell on good ground, and did yield fruit that sprang up and **increased**; and brought forth, some thirty, and some sixty, and some an hundred.

> 8 Finally, some seed fell (alighting) on excellent (in its nature) choice soil, the right soil released the seeds potential, rising up out of the earth (the unseen realm) into the visible (the external), this increase enabled what was hidden to be seen by all, it yielded 30-fold, 60-fold, up to 100-fold (God's choicest and best). (DHP)

My challenge here is simple, why settle for 30-fold when 60-fold is available, why settle for 60-fold when 100-fold is available? Why settle for the good or the acceptable when the perfect will of God is available (See **Romans 12:2**)? Why settle for the outer-court (30-fold), when the Holy Place is available (60-fold), why settle for the Holy Place (60-fold) when the Holy of Holies (Most Holy Place, 100-fold) is available? Selah (think on this)! Allow the seed to complete its process.

13 And he said unto them, **Know** ye not this parable? and how then will ye **know** all parables?

I will do my **DHP** of this verse here but will go into deeper study later in the book.

13 As he continued speaking with them, he stated with the utmost importance of knowing, perceiving and understanding this doctrine and its precepts (the general rule intended to regulate behavior and thought) that he was making known, then he declared, you will struggle to understand/comprehend another parable that I teach in the days to come. (DHP)

The word **"know"** is used two times in this verse in the KJV, however, there are two different Greek words used. The first **"know"** is the Greek word *"eido"* (pronounced "i-do) and references, "perceiving, discerning, discovering with the mind, to inspect and examine, to pay attention to." The second word **"know"** is the Greek word *"ginosko"* (pronounced: ghin-oce-ko) and defines as, "to become acquainted with, to have knowledge." However, the last definition really caught my attention. It is a Jewish idiom for sexual intercourse between a man and a woman. I believe Jesus was letting his disciples know that if they did not get this revelation, this doctrine, truth (parable), if they did not understand, that this one was foundational to the understanding and the unveiling of all the other parables that he would speak.

15 And these are they by the wayside, where the word is sown; but **when they have heard, ssatan cometh immediately**, and **taketh away the word that was sown in their hearts**.

In Mark's account, once they had Jesus alone, they ask him to explain/expound on the parable he had spoken to the multitude, in **Verse 15**, he proceeds in sharing from his teaching earlier in the day.

> **15** Those journeying the well-traveled road (stop just long enough to casually or accidentally hear the message (the seed that was sown, the sayings of God), then, as soon as they hear the instruction, doctrine, and teaching, immediately God's adversary, the enemy, satan comes on the scene to make them doubt in order to remove that which was committed to them, he does not want it to become the center (seat) of their physical and spiritual life. (DHP)

The purpose of this chapter was for us to see and further understand the synoptic gospels versions/writings by His disciples (apostles) on the most important of all parables according to Jesus.

In the rest of this manuscript, we will look primarily at Matthew's gospel (version) of this kingdom parable.

---

1. Gorvadhan Ch, "Msc Botany in Cytogenetics, Molecular Genetics & Biotechnology (college major), Osmania University (Graduated 2020)," Quora, accessed February 24, 2024, https://qr.ae/psT8JL.
2. The Preacher's Complete Homiletic Commentary on the Old Testament, with Critical and Exegetical Notes. By Twenty Distinguished Homiletics, Vol. I, Genesis. J. S. Exell , T. H. Leale. (1892). The Old & New Testament Student, 15(3/4), 179.

CHAPTER FOUR
THE PROBLEM IS NOT THE SEED

1 Peter 1:23 Being born again, not of corruptible seed, but of incorruptible, by the word of God, which liveth and abideth forever.

> **23** Being born anew will reveal a new kingdom mindset, as you walk this out, it will conform you to walk in/and according to God's will, now living the God life (*zoe*), the seed that produced this new life has no corruption in it, none whatsoever, it cannot perish, wither, spoil, become defiled, or come to ruin. This seed is the sayings, decrees, and mandates given/spoken by God himself, his personal discourse, instruction, and doctrine. This seed is active, endless, full of life (His), and will continue and last forever, it has no end, it is eternal. (DHP)

THE ENTIRETY OF GOD CREATING IN THE BOOK OF BEGINNINGS, Genesis (the origin or mode of formation of something) was three-fold, essentially, He **spoke, He made/created, and** He **seeded** (planted). Notice in **Genesis, chapter one (1)**.

HE SPOKE:

3 And God said.
5 And God called (Hebrew "*qara*" pronounced: kaw-raw, which defines as, "to address by name").
6 And God said.
8 And God called.
9 And God said.
10 And God called.
11 And God said.
14 And God said.
20 And God said.
24 And God said.
26 And God said.
29 And God said.

HE MADE/CREATED:

16 And God made (Hebrew "*asah*" pronounced: aw-saw, it means to produce, to press, to squeeze, fashion, and work).
21 And God created.
25 And God made.
27 So God created.

HE SEEDED/PLANTED:

Look at **Genesis, chapter two (2)**.

8 And the LORD God planted (Hebrew "*nata*" pronounced: naw-tah, it translates as, to establish by planting.

1:11 Let the earth bring forth grass, the herb yielding seed, *and* the fruit tree yielding fruit after his kind, whose **seed *is* in itself**.

1:12 And the earth brought forth grass, *and* herb **yielding seed after his kind**, and the tree yielding fruit, whose **seed *was* in itself**.

The Hebrew word for seed is "*zera*" pronounced: zeh-rah, it gives the idea of sowing, then, to bear, conceive, and offspring.

———

THE CLIMAX:

Genesis 1:31

31 And God saw.

In **Genesis 3:15**, God (Himself) speaks the first prophecy continuing the seed concept. Eve was deceived (**1 Timothy 2:14**) as the serpent beguiled (Hebrew: seduced, led her astray). Adam's action was willful disobedience, then God declared:

15 And I will put enmity between thee and the woman, and between thy seed and her seed; it shall bruise thy head, and thou shalt bruise his heel.

15 From this day forward, hatred, hostility and enmity (a deep-rooted hatred) will be seen between you satan and what you manifest, the woman and what she conceives and produces, what comes from/through her will crush what you have now taken the headship of, her offspring will regain what you through your deception has stolen, the only thing noticeable on them will be a bruised heel from walking on you. (DHP)

There are some powerful hidden gems in this prophecy. God speaks of the seed of the woman; however, the woman has no seed, she has a womb, the man has the seed. There was a seed coming through a woman (Mary) who had not known a man intimately. If it were a natural birth and Joseph was the biological father, redemption would not have been available. The seed prophesied was Jesus, the Christ, and through His sinless life and nature, He would fulfill the prophecy by crushing the head of satan, and restoring man back to God's original intent. He would gain headship back that the enemy had stolen.

If I may be so bold, God sowed His Son (seed) into the earth, remember (**John 3:16**), God so loved the world (Greek "**kosmos**" which defines as, "universe, the earth and its inhabitants") that He gave (Greek "**didomi**" pronounced: did-o-mee, which speaks of supplying, furnishing, presenting, and to commission). Gave who? Christ! God's love, not His wrath is the source of redemption for mankind. Paul, the Apostle expounded on this truth to the Corinthian church:

2 Corinthians 9:15

Thanks *be* unto God for his unspeakable gift.

The word *unspeakable* better translates as, "indescribable, inexpressible."

After the creation spoken of in Genesis, chapters one and two, God sets forth the seed principle throughout the scriptures. **Genesis 8:22** reminds us of this truth. The first phrase establishes the duration, then the principle (in ***bold italics*** for emphasis).

22 *While the earth remaineth*, seedtime and harvest, and cold and heat, and summer and winter, and day and night shall not cease.

> **22** As long as the earth (ground, soil) continues, there is/will be sowing time (planting), then what is sown will be harvested (reaped), cool then hot, summer with its fruit then the harvest, morning (day) and night, these will not end, desist, or stop. (DHP)

The seed prophecy of **Genesis 3:15** is again found in the New Testament, in **Galatians 3:16,19,29**. Paul writing to the Galatian church affirms the prophecy spoken by God in the garden and reveals "who" the seed is, and "who" is the offspring of that seed.

Who is the seed?

16 Now to Abraham and his seed were the promises made. He saith not, And to seeds, as of many; but as of one, And to thy seed, which is **Christ**.

> **16** The promised announcement which was a divine assurance of good (blessing) was made to Abraham and his seed (the future, which was yet in his loins, would ultimately reveal a

family, tribe, and nation). What was prophesied and coming would be released through one seed (not many), and the seed had/has a name, Christ, yet the one seed, Christ, would produce a holy nation, why? Because the seed itself was/is holy. (DHP)

19 Wherefore then *serveth* the law? It was added because of transgressions, **till the seed should come** to whom the promise was made; *and it was* ordained by angels in the hand of a mediator.

> **19** So why do you continue as a slave operating under the law, it preceded the prophesied coming seed (Christ), it was added as the result of Adam's sin which released his fallen nature to all of humanity (the law, its effect, and it consequences were made manifest until Christ fulfilled/abolished it, see **Matthew 5:17, Romans 10:4, 2 Corinthians 3:11, Ephesians 2:14-16**), The promised seed came, fulfilled the prophecy, fulfilled the law, then abolished it (the law was a continual reminder that man was in a sinful state since Adam and needed a savior, a deliverer, and a redeemer). (DHP)

One other interesting point, in the Apostle Paul's letter to the Corinthian church, he referred to the law as the "ministry of death" (see **2 Corinthians 3:6,7,9**).

29 And if ye *be* Christ's, then are ye Abraham's seed, and heirs according to the promise.

> **29** Now that you are in Christ, the anointed one, God's only begotten son (**John 3:16**) which differs from Adam, a created son (**Genesis 1:27, Luke 3:38**), and since you came through

Abraham's linage, making you a descendant of his, the prophecy and the promise spoken over/to him includes you, thus making you an heir by right of sonship. (DHP)

The Greek word for begotten is "**monogenēs**" pronounced: mon-og-en-ace, it comes from two Greek words, G3441 and G1096 (Strongs); which means, *only born*, that is, *sole:* - only (begotten, child). The understanding is this, Adam was a created son, he didn't come through natural birth, God Himself created and formed him. On the other hand, Jesus was the only Son born of God. He did come through Mary's womb. She gave Him a body, but God gave Him His blood (which was perfect, sinless, not like that of Adam's after the fall).

Because of His sinless life, His death, burial, and resurrection, the grave could not hold nor keep Him. Why? He was the incorruptible seed spoken of earlier in this chapter. Now because of redemption through Christ, sonship was made available once again to all who would receive Him (the seed), and now many sons can be restored to God's original intent, a glorious son (**Hebrews 2:10**). Now a new creation has come back into existence, and where is Christ (the seed) in correlation to this new man? Once more this new image man manifests the nature, character, and integrity that can only be revealed through the seed's origin (Christ).

WHERE IS THE SEED?

If you enjoy a good mystery movie, you watch it intently looking for any/all clues that would bring to light "whodunnit." After the revealing, it is no longer a mystery because the mystery had been solved.

Colossians 1:26-27

26 *Even* **the mystery which hath been hid from ages** and from generations, **but now is made manifest** to his saints:

27 To whom God would make known what *is* the riches of the glory of this mystery among the Gentiles; which is **Christ in you**, the hope of glory:

> **26** The mystery (the thing which had been hidden, concealed), the very purpose and counsel of God which had been kept secret from nations and the world, but now, at this moment, it is being disclosed (made known) to all of those committed and consecrated to him. (DHP)

> **27** God having pre-determined to release this revelation (at the appointed time, see **Galatians 4:4-5**), this abundant wealth which flowed from God through Christ, the very splendor, glory, and magnificence which had been hidden from humanity (including satan himself) was now made available to every tribe, people group and nation. Are you ready for it? Here it is! It is Christ, our Messiah, and his anointing (given to him from the Father), all of this is now **IN** you, his new creation man, in seed form, waiting to be developed, grown, pruned, watered, and fertilized to reveal Christ through you in the same manner that He revealed the Father through himself, His son. (DHP)

SOME FINAL THOUGHTS AS WE CLOSE OUT THIS CHAPTER.

Jesus spoke some powerful thoughts (actually, referring to Himself, His purpose and mission) in John's gospel:

John 12:24

24 Verily, verily, I say unto you, Except a corn of wheat fall into the ground and die, it abideth alone: but if it die, it bringeth forth much fruit.

> **24** From this very truth I speak to you, unless a grain (a kernel of seed) falls (descends from a higher place to a lower place) and is planted, buried into the earth (ground) and dies, until it dies, the one seed remains alone, without offspring, then at death, something incredible and amazing happens, literally a miracle. The seed (grain) that died, and then out of death brings forth and produces life, great in multitude, in quantity. (DHP)

Notes from Adam Clarke's commentary:

Except a corn of wheat fall into the ground and die - Our Lord compares himself to a grain of wheat; his death, to a grain sown and decomposed in the ground; his resurrection, to the blade which springs up from the dead grain; which grain, thus dying, brings forth an abundance of fruit. I must die to be glorified; and, unless I am glorified, I cannot establish a glorious Church of Jews and Gentiles upon earth. In comparing himself thus to a grain of wheat, our Lord shows us:

1. The cause of his death - the order of God, who had rated the redemption of the world at this price; as in nature he had attached

41

the multiplication of the corn to the death or decomposition of the grain.

2. The end of his death - the redemption of a lost world; the justification, sanctification, and glorification of men: as the multiplication of the corn is the end for which the grain is sown and dies.

3. The mystery of his death, which we must credit without being able fully to comprehend, as we believe the dead grain multiplies itself, and we are nourished by that multiplication, without being able to comprehend how it is done.[1]

There is another side to the seed concept, all seeds are not good, weeds are also seeds. Recently I was speaking at a yearly conference in Texas with a dear friend of mine, Apostle Anthony Turner, and he made this statement that truly spoke to me, and I believe it will you also. He said, *"If you don't deal with it as a seed, one day you will have to deal with it as a tree."*

———

MY LONGTIME FRIEND, RON KIDMAN, FROM MICHIGAN SENT ME the following while writing this manuscript. I copy it with his permission:

GROWTH:

Germination is the process a seed goes through when it "wakes up" (when we come to ourselves, hello prodigals) from its dormant state and starts to grow. Seeds are self-contained systems that contain most of what they need to get themselves started, but there are three important triggers that kick off germination: AIR, WATER, and HEAT. I believe we need these also to grow as sons.

WATER:

John 4:10

Jesus answered and said unto her, If thou knewest the gift of God, and who it is that saith to thee, Give me to drink; thou wouldest have asked of him, and he would have given thee living water.

John 7:37-38

37 On the last day of the feast, the great day, Jesus stood up and cried out, "if anyone thirsts, let him come to me and drink."

38 Whoever believes in me, as the scripture has said, "Out of his heart will flow rivers of living water" (ESV).

AIR:

Genesis 2:7

7 Then the Lord God formed the man of dust from the ground and breathed into his nostrils the breath of life, and the man became a living creature (ESV).

John 20:22

22 And when he had said this, he breathed on them and said to them, "receive the Holy Spirit" (ESV).

HEAT:

The Holy Spirit is the Holy Fire that burns within us, the Old Testament was used for the sacrifice, it represented God's presence, in the New Testament, we are called to be a living sacrifice.

Romans 12:1-2

1 I appeal to you therefore, brothers, by the mercies of God, to present your bodies as a living sacrifice, holy and acceptable to God, which is your spiritual worship.

2 Do not be conformed to this world, but be transformed by the renewal of your mind, that by testing you may discern what is the will of God, what is good and acceptable and perfect (ESV).

Luke 24:32

32 They said to each other, "did not our hearts burn within us while he talked to us on the road, while he opened to us the scriptures" (ESV)?

Acts 2:1-3

1 When the day of Pentecost arrived, they were all together in one place.

2 And suddenly there came from heaven a sound like a mighty rushing wind, and it filled the entire house where they were sitting.

3 And divided tongues as of fire appeared to them and rested on each one of them (ESV).

Thanks so much Ron for your thoughts my covenant brother and friend (heart-to-heart).

————

A FEW MORE FINAL THOUGHTS AS WE CLOSE OUT THIS CHAPTER. For a seed to grow into what its DNA declares it is, there are a few **musts** for this to happen. The soil it is sown into must have the proper **nutrients**, the right amount of **water**, **sunlight** (in our circles, we would call it SON-light, the right amount of **heat** (temperature), and final **room to grow** and **time to grow** (SELAH)! Remember **Genesis 8:22**, Seed-Time-Harvest. (In the natural, the soil is the major source of the nutrients needed to grow and become a plant.

The three main ingredients in the soil are nitrogen (N), phosphorus (P) and potassium (K). For the spiritual seed to grow and mature, there must be the initial planting, the process of dying (to one's self), plenty of water (Word of God), an ongoing intimate relationship with the Son (sun) and the right amount of heat (which is two-fold), first, to burn away anything that is not biblically nutrient-based that could hinder the seed's growth and process, and secondly, to continue to aid the development of the seed into its designated DNA.

————

1. Clarke, A. (1869). Clarke's Commentary: The Holy Bible, containing the Old and New Testaments: The Text printed from the most correct copies of the Present Authorized Translation, including the marginal readings and parallel texts, with a Commentary and Critical Notes.

CHAPTER FIVE
CONTINUING THOUGHTS ON THE SEED

In Mark's account of the parable of the Sower, he states in **Mark 4:4b**, "and **the fowls of the air** came and devoured it up." Later that day, when the disciples had Jesus alone, they ask him to expound on the parable further. In **Verse 15**, he makes known and identifies who/what the fowl of the air is, "but when they have heard, **satan cometh immediately**, and taketh away the word that was sown in their hearts." **Luke's** account uses almost the exact wording in **Luke 8:5**, "and it was trodden down, and the fowls of the air devoured it."

The interesting note in Mark and Luke's writing is that the fowl came at once (right away) to devour the seed. The Greek word for devour is "*katesthiō*" (pronounced: kat-es-thee'-o" which uses words/phrases like, "to strip one of his goods, to ruin by infliction and injury, to consume, to make a prey of." As Jesus responds to the disciple's request, he reveals the identity of the fowl in **Verse 15** as satan and he comes immediately!

Notes from John Gill's Commentary on **Mark 4:4**:

"and the fowls of the air came and devoured it up; the devils, who have their abode in the air, especially the prince of the posse of them; and the Syriac version reads it in the singular number, "and the fowl came"; that ravenous bird of prey, Satan, who goes about seeking what he may devour; and for this purpose attends where the word is preached, to hinder its usefulness as much as in him lies."

The Greek word for **satan** is *"satanas"* (pronounced: sat-an-as') and describes him as, "an adversary (one who opposes another in purpose or act), the inveterate adversary of God and Christ, circumventing men by his wiles, the accuser, the devil." The Greek word for **immediately** is *"eutheōs"* (pronounced: yoo-theh'-oce), it references something that happens, "at once, straight way, instantly." If he is the adversary of God and Christ as defined above, then he is also the ecclesia's adversary, the CHRIST-ones made in his image and likeness, those once again reflecting the Father and the Son as Adam did before his fall. Not only does the enemy want to hinder you from "**hearing**" the seed (Word), but his plan is also to stop the seed from being "**received**" in the correct soil, so the root process never occurs.

When a seed is exposed to the proper conditions, water and oxygen are taken in through the seed coat. The embryo's cell starts to enlarge. Then, the seed coat breaks open and the root emerges (downward-my thoughts) first, followed by the shoot (upward-my thoughts) that contains the leaves and the stem. Sunlight (illumination, revelation, impartation-my thoughts) supports the germination process by warming the soil.[1]

I believe the **Genesis 3:15** prophecy from God himself of the coming seed who would conquer satan and restore what he had stolen, sonship with all its privileges, and bring man back to God's original intent and purpose. This profound declaration immediately after Adam's fall can be found in two key passages of scripture in the New Testament (not necessarily in chronological order).

REFERENCE #1

Matthew 16:13-20

13 When Jesus came into the coasts of Caesarea Philippi, he asked his disciples, saying, Whom do men say that I the Son of man am?

14 And they said, Some *say that thou art* John the Baptist: some, Elias; and others, Jeremias, or one of the prophets.

15 He saith unto them, But whom say ye that I am?

16 And Simon Peter answered and said, **Thou art the Christ**, the Son of the living God.

17 And Jesus answered and said unto him, Blessed art thou, Simon Barjona: **for flesh and blood hath not revealed *it* unto thee,** but my Father which is in heaven.

18 And I say also unto thee, That thou art Peter, and **upon this rock I will build my church**; and the gates of hell shall not prevail against it.

19 And I will give unto thee the keys of the kingdom of heaven: and whatsoever thou shalt bind on earth shall be bound in heaven: and whatsoever thou shalt loose on earth shall be loosed in heaven.

20 Then charged he his disciples that they should tell no man that he was Jesus the Christ.

———

WHILE ENTERING THE COASTS OF CAESAREA PHILIPPI, JESUS asks His disciples a question. *"Who do men say that I the Son of man am?"* I am not necessarily convinced that Jesus was greatly concerned about what others were saying concerning himself. I believe he used the first question to get to the real question. *"Whom say ye that I am?"*

Simon Peter's answer was profound on many levels, first, as we look at the life of Peter. He often had a way of opening his mouth, inserting his foot, and chewing, as they say, eating your own words. In this dialogue with Jesus, it shows both sides of his two names (natures), Simon (reed) and Peter (a rock or stone). In his first statement in this passage, Peter makes known a previously unknown (mystery), revealing a long-time hidden truth that would be brought to the light that very day. In his second statement, Simon works through him again, then Jesus rebukes him and called him satan. If we are totally honest with ourselves, we have all been guilty of speaking out of both sides of our mouth on more than one occasion.

Peter answers Jesus's question in **verse 16**, "And Simon Peter answered and said, Thou art **the Christ, the Son of the living God**."

You are the anointed Messiah, the Son of the one and only true and living God, He is superior and carries the pre-eminence, there is none like him nor above him (You are the revealed **Genesis 3:15** seed of promise. (DHP).

This was the first time this name was revealed and used in the New Testament and never used in the Old Testament. At the climax of that prophecy being released through Peter, Jesus states with resounding applause, "Peter, you did not get this through the flesh and blood doctrines and traditions of men, this came from the highest source and voice there is, My Father laid open and uncovered what had been covered and veiled since the garden, showing you My true identity and purpose, the **Genesis 3:15** seed [my thoughts]."

Now, here is why I believe this is true and it fits in line with other scriptures and principles. In the beginning of this chapter, we looked in-depth at the words, **satan** and **immediately**. The concept is in the quickness of the enemy coming in to steal the seed, truth, and revelation that was made known. Why? Before the seed, truth and revelation can take root.

After Peter receives and reveals this truth, Jesus expounds on it in **verses 18-19**:

> **18** You are ***Petros*** (a piece of the rock) and as my father discloses this truth to you that I am the rock, ***Petra*** (the seed), I will use you (***petros***), a piece of the rock to announce, proclaim, share, preach, teach, and build my church (***ekklesia***), and even though the counsels and evil purposes of hell itself will come against and try to stop this truth from being seen, and it's

foundation laid, their strength is inferior and will not be able to prevail or overpower it at all. (**DHP**)

19 I am giving to you (*petros*) the keys (the instruments that possess the power to open and shut) to release and build from the pattern (my heavenly kingdom) into the earthly kingdom that I have given you dominion, power, and rule over. Whatever you prohibit and permit, whatever you bind will be forbidden, whatever you lose, it will be done. When you release these kingdom tools and principles, you will have access to heavens divine authority than comes from the creator, God himself. (DHP)

After Peter's revealing of the promised seed, the Christ, Jesus begins to unfold what He must go through to accomplish and fulfill the prophecy, but He also tells them, you now know this, however, it is not yet time to disclose it to others. He goes on to talk about the upcoming events, Jerusalem, the coming confrontation of the religious system of the day, the priests, elders, and scribes which will ultimately meet with His death, the crucifixion (which would fulfill **Genesis, 3:15, John 1:29, Revelation 13:8**).

Remember, once the seed is sown, its DNA, purpose and potential destiny are revealed. That is why satan comes immediately, and it was no different on that day when Peter received the revelation. Notice his response to Jesus disclosing his purpose, and he must go through to fulfill it:

Matthew 16:21-22

21 From that time forth began Jesus to shew unto his disciples, how that he must go unto Jerusalem, and suffer many things of the elders and chief priests and scribes, and be killed, and be raised again the third day.

22 Then Peter took him, and began to rebuke him, saying, Be it far from thee, Lord: this shall not be unto thee.

> **21** After Peter's God-given revelation as to Jesus being the Christ (the seed), Jesus set a precedent (a priority of importance, order, and rank) that day sharing with his disciples, that to fulfill his purpose, and accomplish his mission, he had to go through Jerusalem, and that he would come under great persecution and suffering at the hands of the city's elders, chief priests, and scribes. The result would be his death, but ultimately, he would resurrect from death, hell, and the grave on the third day. (DHP)

> **22** Immediately Simon interrupted him, took him aside and rebuked him sharply (forbidding this to happen) saying, "Lord (Master), NO, NEVER, by any means will this happen. [If you noticed, in this verse I changed his name back to Simon (reed) as he was now not operating from the revelation given to Peter (rock) but one who was moved by his mind, will and emotions.] (DHP)

Right then, at that moment, Jesus wasted no time, He did not want the revelation (seed) uprooted that had been planted in Peter from the Father. How powerful and direct was His response to him:

Matthew 16:23

23 Get thee behind me, Satan: thou art an offence unto me: for thou savourest not the things that be of God, but those that be of men.

23 Peter, you have sided with my adversary (satan who opposes me accomplishing and fulfilling my purpose and destiny), get these thoughts from in front of you to behind you, the enemy now operating through you is trying to impede (prevent) the very thing from happening that I was sent to fulfill. Peter, once again, your present language is revealing that you are not operating out of your spirit, but through your flesh (mind, will, and emotions) as much of mankind continually does. (DHP)

Jesus's adversary, satan, operating through Peter who had just received the revelation came immediately to steal!

REFERENCE #2

Matthew 3:13,16,17

13 Then cometh Jesus from Galilee to Jordan unto John, to be baptized of him.

16 And Jesus, when he was baptized, went up straightway out of the water: and, lo, **the heavens were opened** unto him, and he saw **the Spirit of God descending** like a dove, and lighting upon him:

17 And lo **a voice from heaven, saying, This is my beloved Son**, in whom I am well pleased.

John is baptizing Jesus in the Jordan river, from 12 years of age until now (30 years of age) it seems as if Jesus lived in obscurity as nothing is really recorded in the gospels, yet we know according to Luke's account that He "grew in wisdom, stature, and favor with God and man" (**Luke 2:52**). He was growing, going through His own process, preparation, and development for the 3.5 years of ministry that was in front of Him.

As Jesus was coming up out of the waters of baptism, the heavens open, the Holy Spirit descends upon Him and the voice of the Father speaks, "This is My beloved Son." I believe in light of what we have penned so far which came through study, preparing the notes for this manuscript, and divine inspiration by the Holy Spirit, this is another reference (announcement) of the one who would fulfill the prophecy of **Genesis 3:15**.

——

ON A SIDE NOTE, A THOUGHT TO CONSIDER FOR THOSE WHO MAY not be students of the Word (studiers). Jesus's public ministry began at baptism (age 30), yet there are no references or occurrences recorded in the gospels of Him performing one miracle before this day. Why? I believe the answer in found in the scriptures:

#1

"The Spirit of God descending like a dove, and lighting upon Him" (**Matthew 3:16b**). There is no reference before here of the Holy Spirit being on Jesus or working with/through Him.

This was the third person of the Trinity, descending upon Him in the form of a dove, The dove, among the Jews, was the symbol of purity of heart, harmlessness, and gentleness, compare, **Psalm_55:6-7**. The form chosen here was doubtless an emblem of the innocence, meekness, and tenderness of the Saviour. The gift of the Holy Spirit, in this manner, was the public approbation of Jesus, **John_1:33**, and a sign of His being set apart to the office of the Messiah. We are not to suppose that there was any change done in the moral character of Jesus, but only that He was publicly set apart to His work, and solemnly approved by God in the office to which He was appointed (Albert Barnes commentary).

The Holy Spirit is the oil, the anointing. Jesus had to be anointed to do the greater works, signs, wonders, and miracles. As you read this, you may be saying NO! But wait, there is more. Another verse some may have never read or need to be reminded of.

#2

Acts 10:38

How **God anointed Jesus of Nazareth with the Holy Ghost** and with power: who went about doing good, and healing all that were oppressed of the devil; for God was with him.

38 God the Father, the first person of the trinity, consecrated Jesus to his Messianic assignment, furnishing him with the necessary powers for its administration, the Holy Ghost (Spirit), releasing his strength, power, and ability to him and to operate through him. His journey of public ministry for the next 3.5 years had begun, he did good, bestowing benefits (Greek meaning-philanthropic, one who seeks to promote the welfare of others, giving generously to good causes) on the people, bringing them the gift of salvation, healing them, applying the cure for sin and the curse, making them whole, setting free the oppressed, those under the control and exploited by the enemy, God now working with/through him. (DHP)

ANOTHER PROOF:

Matthew 4:1

1 Then was Jesus **led up of the Spirit** into the wilderness to be tempted of the devil.

To be led by the Spirit, he had to be endowed with the Spirit. God announced in **Matthew 3:17**, Jesus was His Son (the seed prophesied in **Genesis 3:15**). He was now empowered to do, fulfill, and accomplish the will of His Father. This may challenge our thinking some, but according to **verse one**, God did the leading through the Holy Spirit, the devil did the tempting.

The phrase, "**led up**" in the Greek describes one who navigates from a lower place to a higher place. The Holy Spirit would lead/navigate/be with him through the temptation. The Greek word for **tempted** is "*peirazō*" (pronounced: pi-rad'-zo) which translates as, "to test, to scrutinize, to entice, to examine, to test for the purpose of finding out one's qualities, what they think, how they behave themselves, and finally their faith and character."

What God had just declared over Him would be immediately tested. Remember, how quickly does the enemy come to steal/challenge the seed? Immediately! An interesting thought, in Matthew's gospel (**Matthew 4:1-3**) and Luke's gospel (**Luke 4:1-3**), that the devil came and began the temptation after the forty days, not during the forty days. After forty days of fasting (dealing with the flesh), and prayer (intimacy with the Father), the devil decides to show up. In my opinion, he was forty days late. Notice the enemy's question during the day of testing? It was the same question.

Matthew 4:3

"If thou be the Son of God…"

Matthew 4:6

"If thou be the Son of God…"

In light of this manuscript and taking two complete chapters to reveal the **Genesis 3:15** seed prophecy, I am convinced throughout the Bible's history, satan **DID NOT** know that Jesus was the fulfillment of that prophetic word. Why? Even in many books of the Old Testament, there are examples of the enemy causing death, darkness, evil and corruption but the prophecy made it through. The enemy was wondering, pondering, was it Noah **(Genesis 6:1)**? Was it Moses **(Exodus 1:22)**? Was it David, Gideon, Samson, or another?

Each time the seed (promise) made it through for it was for a yet appointed time. When Peter revealed the Christ and God revealed his Son (seed), it was no longer a mystery. Peter revealed it, Simon tried to talk Jesus out of it. God announced it, satan came immediately to question, to conquer, to see that the seed never got planted, or at best, uprooted. But God's prophecy would come to pass, the lamb would literally be slain (as it always had happened in the mind of God before He framed the world).

The seed Jesus would be planted, die, and resurrected, just like the seed's designed DNA. Remember these verses:

1 Corinthians 2:7-8

7 But we speak the wisdom of God in a mystery, *even* the hidden *wisdom,* which God ordained before the world unto our glory:

8 Which none of the princes of this world knew: for had they known *it,* they would not have crucified the Lord of glory.

God's enemy fell right into his plan and had no discernment as to the outcome. Each time satan as the question, "if you be the Son of God?" I believe he had a two-fold purpose, he wanted to know, and he wanted Jesus to question it.

A final thought in closing, the last statement in the temptation was an offer from the devil, look closely:

Matthew 4:8-9

8 Again, the devil taketh him up into an exceeding high mountain, and **sheweth him all the kingdoms of the world, and the glory of them;**

9 **And saith unto him, All these things will I give thee**, if thou wilt fall down and worship me.

JESUS **DID NOT** QUESTION OR CHALLENGE IF THE KINGDOMS belonged to him, at that moment, they were still under his control from the fall of Adam. They had to be his or it would not have been a legitimate temptation. Selah! The truth was if Jesus had given in and worshiped him, he would have not given them to Him, and mankind would have been doomed for eternity.

Jesus's answer was:

Matthew 4:10

10 Then saith Jesus unto him, Get thee hence, Satan: for it is written, Thou shalt worship the Lord thy God, and him only shalt thou serve.

Luke's account states that the devil departed the failed temptation for a "**season**" (**Luke 4:13**). If the enemy came at Jesus, the seed, more than once, rest assured, he will come at you to question, challenge the prophetic words spoken over you which are tied to your purpose and destiny, he will try and cause you to doubt, his plan never changed, he wants to steal the seed, kill its purpose and destroy its destiny.

I declare over you right now, I prophesy that your latter shall be greater than your former, your seed is tied to your calling and has a kingdom purpose, it will not be uprooted. The eyes of your understanding are gaining new enlightenment at this very moment, your past will not dictate your future, better is the end of a thing than the beginning, it is not how you start, it is how you finish, and you will finish strong, you will finish your race, you will cross the finish line, you will get a winner's wreath. Your tears will turn into laughter, your sorrow into joy, your failures into victories, your best is yet to come. It is NOT over, God, not satan, has the last word.

Some final thoughts as we close out this chapter. In the Apostle Paul's letter to the Church in Ephesus, he continues to expound to another church the mystery, the revealing to his ekklesia, the manifold wisdom of God concerning the purpose of Christ, the prophesied seed once again in **Genesis 3:15**. The evidence is unarguable, undeniable, unquestionable and undisputable throughout the scriptures that the prophesy was/is fulfilled.

Ephesians 3:9-11

9 And to make all *men* see what *is* the fellowship of the mystery, which from the beginning of the world hath been hid in God, who created all things by Jesus Christ:

10 To the intent that now unto the principalities and powers in heavenly *places* might be known by the church the manifold wisdom of God,

11 According to the eternal purpose which he purposed in Christ Jesus our Lord:

> **9** Now, all of mankind, the entire human race can receive this spiritual enlightenment, they can be brought to the light and perceive clearly this dispensation of what once was a mystery, hidden in God from the world's beginning until the appointed time which would move mankind from a "creation" to a "new creation" in and through Christ, the promised seed. (DHP)
>
> **10** In order that God's purpose and its result will now be made manifest, even to the angelic hosts surrounding the throne and the Ekklesia (church), God, unfolding his multifaceted wisdom (supreme intelligence) on what was once a mystery (his hidden purpose). (DHP)
>
> **11** His plan and purpose throughout the ages, past, present, and future was made known, seen, and revealed through the unveiling of his son (the seed) Jesus. Jesus released the seed Christ, the anointing (**Galatians 3:16**), into his earth (us), then after the death, burial, and resurrection, ascended into the heavens, sat down and the right hand of his father, and began

interceding for the saints (us) that the revelation would be seen, received, and lived out on the earth. (DHP)

Consider this: Jesus left the planet, Christ **NEVER** did!

———

I HAVE A TWO-VOLUME SET CALLED, "WEEKLY WORD STUDIES WITH THE DOC." IT CONTAINS ONE HUNDRED WORDS AND PHRASES IN THE OLD & NEW TESTAMENTS. IT IS DESIGNED TO STUDY ONE PER WEEK (NOT LIKE THE TRADITIONAL DAILY DEVOTIONAL). IN VOLUME ONE, WEEK 22, I WROTE ON THE WORD, "SEED" AND THOUGHT IT SHOULD BE ADDED TO THE END OF THAT CHAPTER, ENJOY. YOU CAN ORDER ONE OR BOTH VOLUMES THROUGH OUR MINISTRY

———

WEEK 22 PRESCRIPTION...SEED: EXCERPT FROM "WORD STUDIES WITH THE DOC"

This week's **WORD** is **seed**. I was amazed to find over two hundred and fifty references in the Bible. Beginning with the "book of beginnings" Genesis, then woven as a thread in a garment, being found in almost every book ending with Revelation. There is basically one Hebrew word for seed in the Old Testament and one in the Greek in the New Testament.

The Hebrew word is "*zera*" (pronounced: zeh-rah) which describes something that is sown, yields, bears, conceives, and produces. The Greek word is "*sperma*" (pronounced: sper-mah)

which translates as "the grain or kernel which contains within itself the germ of the future plant. In Genesis, God created this earth with "**and God said**" then He placed seed within much of His creation and declared that what He had created would yield/produce because its "seed was in itself." (**Genesis 1:11-12**)

The entire plan of redemption can be summed up in this concept: God saw a need in the earth, so He planted a seed, **HIS SON** into it and the rest is...WELL...you know the story and the answer.

In the Old Testament, God began with the seed principle and the earth began to produce. In the New Testament, God's plan was to sow the seed of His Son into the hearts and lives of humanity (if you will allow me...EARTH). Every seed is designed with its own DNA to produce after its own kind. The seed of "...Christ in you..." (**Colossians 1:27**) is a master blueprint to produce **His GLORY** in/and through you to the world.

The Psalmist David proclaimed that "...the earth is the LORD'S, and the fullness thereof..." (**Psalm 24:1**). Our earth (life) is supposed to be fertile ground where all that God has planted/formed in us can be harvested for His Glory. The only thing holding back the coming of the Lord is that His earth (us) must manifest the precious fruit (**James 5:7**).

You will bloom where He plants you, you will produce a harvest that will bring Him much glory. Your destiny, your calling, your abundance, everything **you are** and everything **you need** is ALREADY in you in seed form. As long as the "...earth remaineth..." (You) the ability for "seedtime and harvest" exists. (**Genesis 8:22**)

God has already sown into your life all that pertains to life and godliness. Your future is contained within your earth, and I can promise you that your future is bright. Let the rains of His Spirit come, let the light of His Word reveal and expose, the seed in you will germinate and His harvest will be produced in/and through you. I guess you could say, "It's always been a **seed** thing."

His servant releasing His seed,

Doc

Think twice before you speak, because your words and influence will plant the seed of either success or failure in the mind of another.

Napoleon Hill

---

1. Mary Beth Bennett, "Germinating Seeds," WVU Extension Service (February 1, 2021), accessed February 24, 2024, https://extension.wvu.edu/ lawn-gardening-pests/news/2021/02/01/germinating- seeds#:~:text=When%20a%20seed%20is%20ex- posed,process%20by%20warming%20the%20soil.

CHAPTER SIX
THE PARABLE OF THE SOWER

IN THE FIRST FIVE CHAPTERS, WE UPROOTED SOME WRONG mindsets, misconceptions, and even bad foundations that were poured from the traditions of men and religious systems that are void of the kingdom message being revealed and released into the earth.

Jesus taught many parables throughout His earthly time of ministry, only twelve of them started with the phrase, "the kingdom of heaven is like." This parable is the only one of the kingdom parables where Jesus made this profound statement in Mark's gospel.

Mark 4:13

13 And he said unto them, **Know ye not this parable? and how then will ye know all parables**?

13 Jesus spoke to his disciples and said, "If you do not perceive, discern, inspect and examine this kingdom parable (this earthly story with a heavenly meaning), if you do not become acquainted with this parable intimately to the point of knowing and understanding it, as it is foundational, by what means will you be able to understand the other parables which I will reveal?" (DHP)

The Parable of the Sower & the Seed

In Matthew's gospel, he pens his version of the Sower Parable. We find Jesus sitting by the seaside, a great multitude gathers around Him, then He steps into a ship, sits down, and begins His discourse on this kingdom parable.

Matthew 13:3-9

3 And he spake many things unto them in parables, saying, Behold, a sower went forth to sow;

> 3 Then Jesus began to teach them regularly concerning kingdom doctrines and precepts (earthly stories with heavenly meanings), all which portray the nature and history of God's kingdom, comparing the natural and the spiritual, he began his message with, "a Sower (farmer), ones who scatters seed, released it into the earth." (DHP)

4 And when he sowed, some *seeds* fell by the way side, and the fowls came and devoured them up:

Some seeds fell by the way-side - That is, the hard "path" or headland, which the plow had not touched, and where there was no opportunity for it to sink into the earth (Albert Barnes Commentary).

> **4** He released (sowed) the seed and as it descended, it first landed upon a ground that the plow had not touched, so, because of the soil's hardened (unplowed) condition, the opportunity to sink into the earth was not there, then the seed laying exposed in the open made easy access to the fowls (the seed's enemy) to make its appearance, devour, consume, and eat the seed not meant for it. (DHP)

5 Some fell upon stony places, where they had not much earth: and forthwith they sprung up, because they had no deepness of earth:

> **5** Some seed fell on rocky areas where there were more rocks and stones than earth, then, almost immediately a shoot (the above ground part of the plant) sprouted up because there was not sufficient soil or moisture from the soil. (DHP)

6 And when the sun was up, they were scorched; and because they had no root, they withered away.

> **6** When the rays of heat from the sun hit the seed on the ground full of rocks, it withered away quickly having no depth of good soil thus no depth of roots. (DHP)

7 And some fell among thorns; and the thorns sprung up, and choked them:

7 Some of the Sower's seed fell on thorns (a briar bush-a woody, thorny prickly stem), the part of the field (soil) where the thorns and prickly shrubs had not been properly cleared and destroyed, so the thorns grew and strangled, stifled, and suffocated the seed and its potential. (DHP)

They grew with the grain, crowded it, shaded it, exhausted the earth, and thus choked it (Albert Barnes Commentary).

8 But other fell into good ground, and brought forth fruit, some an hundredfold, some sixtyfold, some thirtyfold.

8 Finally, some seed fell upon beautiful (good, excellent in its nature and characteristics, well adapted to reveal the seed's purpose and DNA) soil, manifesting (producing) fruit, one hundred times as much (as the original seed planted), sixty times as much, and thirty times as much. (DHP)

9 Who hath ears to hear, let him hear.

9 Hear (perceive with your mind), understand, and know (become intimate with) with kingdom parable you have just heard. (DHP)

It is important to know and understand that this parable is **NOT** about **four types of seed**. It is about **four types of soil**.

In this parable, I believe the Lord reveals and expounds on a major kingdom key to experience the fruit that is available to His sons and daughters, the importance of the soil.

———

THE PURPOSE OF PARABLES

In **Verse 10**, the disciples question Jesus purpose in teaching in parables:

10 And the disciples came, and said unto him, Why speakest thou unto them in parables?

> **10** Jesus disciples (students) approached him and ask, "why do you teach the people in metaphors and comparisons (aphorisms-an observation that contains a general truth)?" (DHP)

His answer to them unveils a side of Him that many without study and research would seriously question.

11 He answered and said unto them, Because **it is given unto you to know the mysteries of the kingdom of heaven**, but to them it is not given.

> **11** He answered their proposed question by saying, "these kingdom keys (truths) have been delivered (entrusted unto you), these hidden and concealed truths are being given unto you (because of your pursuit) but not to the masses or crowds whose pursuit of me is not the same (will explain this last statement further into this chapter). (DHP)

The Greek word for **mysteries** is *"musterion"* (pronounced: moos-tay-ree-on), it describes a "hidden thing, religious secrets, confided only to the initiated and not to ordinary mortals, not obvious to the understanding, a hidden purpose or counsel of God: the secret counsels which govern God in dealing with the righteous, which are hidden from ungodly and wicked men but plain to the godly." (Thayer's)

Here is a challenge to all that are reading this manuscript: The Kingdom message and its keys are revealed to the teachable, the hungry, those pursuing righteousness, **NOT** the average church attendee, who goes occasionally, never brings their Bible, let alone a notebook, often there for wrong motives, to pass out their business cards, to build their downline, to get free babysitting services…,I think you get the point. Selah!!!

In **Verse 12**, the Lord seems to get more intense in His explanation to them:

12 For whosoever hath, to him shall be given, and he shall have more abundance: but whosoever hath not, from him shall be taken away even that he hath.

> **12** Those who already have (possess) because of their pursuit, more will be bestowed, supplied, and furnished, entrusted, and committed to them to the point of abundance (overflow), then whoever has little to nothing because of their lack of pursuit, they will eventually over time lose that too. (DHP)

Notice the phrase in **Verse 12**, "whosoever hath." Hath what? Stay in the context of what Jesus was teaching. **He who has knowledge of the mysteries of the kingdom** (that answer is found in **Verse 11** above). He told his disciples that these kingdom keys were given to them to **KNOW**. The Greek word **know** is "*ginosko*" (pronounced: ghin-oce-sko) which translates as, "to perceive, to understand where you can speak." It is also a

Jewish idiom for sexual intercourse between a man and a woman.

I believe that it takes this type of spiritual intimacy with God, His Word (Jesus) and His Spirit (Holy Spirit) to become intimate with these keys and truths. It will be a life-long endeavor on our part for these kingdom truths/secrets to be revealed, imparted into our lives, and lived out. The more we pursue Him, the move of Himself he reveals.

If you do not want to pursue Him or them (the keys), do not worry, He will not reveal, tell, or show you. I can almost hear someone saying, "WELL. I do not believe that!" Okay, let us look at a very familiar verse of scripture that many can probably quote.

2 Timothy 2:15

15 Study to shew thyself approved unto God, a workman that needeth not to be ashamed, rightly dividing the word of truth.

> **15** Give diligence, labor, endeavor earnestly in your study, this will gain the Father's approval, be a spiritual laborer (workman), no shame will ever come to the one with this type of pursuit, the result will be this, you will stay on course, you will keep your path straight and finally be able to teach direct and correct. (DHP)

The Greek word for **study** is "*spoudazo*" (pronounced: spoo-dad-zo) which defines as, "to be diligent, prompt or earnest to do, to exert oneself." Only this type of person can truly rightly divide, a studier (not a reader).

More insight into our responsibility:

John 8:31-32

31 Then said Jesus to those Jews which believed on him, If ye continue in my word, *then* are ye my disciples indeed;

> **31** Jesus directed his words to the Jews that believed on and had confidence in him, "If you continue, abide and dwell in my word (sayings, mandates, and decrees), that is evidence that you are my disciples (students, learners, pupils). (DHP)

The Greek word for **continue** is *"meno"* (pronounced: men-o) and it means, "to remain, abide, to sojourn, tarry, to not depart, to continue to be present, to be held, kept, to remain as one, not to become another or different."

I believe that **Verse 31** is the acid-test of our faith and trust in the Lord and His word. **John 14:21** acted upon with more than just words prove our commitment and faith. "He that hath my commandments, and keepeth them, he it is that loveth me: and he that loveth me shall be loved of my Father, and I will love him, and will **manifest** myself to him." I love the promise given here to those who "loves him with actions keeping his commandments (being a doer of the word)." His promise is, "I will manifest myself to those." The Greek word for **manifest** is *"emphanizō"* (pronounced em-fan-id'-zo) which defines as, "to appear, to exhibit (in person), to reveal."

32 And ye shall know the truth, and the truth shall make you free.

32 Your pursuit as a student of my word will make known to you what was previously unknown, the intimacy you will have with me through my word, then acted upon will set you at liberty, it will free you from sin's dominion, ultimately liberating you completely. (DHP)

James continues to expand on this truth of "hearing **and** doing" in his writings.

James 1:22-25

22 But be ye doers of the word, and not hearers only, deceiving your own selves.

22 Act on the word, apply the word, be active with it and obey it, do not just hear (listen), as this can/will lead to delusion (false beliefs or judgments about eternal truths), and ultimately self-deception (false reasonings), being deceived and not knowing that you are. (DHP)

23 For if any be a hearer of the word, and not a doer, he is like unto a man beholding his natural face in a glass:

23 Those who only hear (listen) but never apply what they have heard, they illustrate someone who stands in front of a mirror only long enough to see all the features (attributes or aspects) then, because they don't remain in the mirror which images the things they have heard, the images and impressions which are meant to change them all vanish. (DHP)

24 For he beholdeth himself, and goeth his way, and straightway forgetteth what manner of man he was.

72

24 As long as he remains looking into the mirror, he continues to see what God sees, because he didn't stay focused on the image in the mirror long enough to where the image becomes engraved in his mind, immediately upon turning away, the image leaves his mind, and he forgets the quality, greatness and excellence of what he had just seen. (DHP)

25 But whoso looketh into the perfect law of liberty, and continueth *therein,* he being not a forgetful hearer, but a doer of the work, this man shall be blessed in his deed.

25 Those who inspect and look carefully into the finished work, revealing God's will through his word will live in true liberty (freedom), then remain, abide, continue there, and you will not forget what you have heard and seen, you will become employed in his kingdom and you, and others will know it by the blessings released through your diligence. (DHP)

Back to the parable in Matthew's gospel:

Matthew 13:16

16 But blessed *are* your eyes, for they see: and your ears, for they hear.

16 You are fortunate, supremely blessed because your eyes (literally and figuratively, the eyes of your mind and understanding) have seen the evidence, the confirmation, the fruit of teaching these kingdom principles and keys, you have been endowed with the ability to consider and perceive what is being said. (DHP)

What did the disciples see and hear? The mysteries of the kingdom were revealed unto them. I trust that you realize how blessed you truly are and the potential you have inside of you when you attend a true ekklesia (church) that teaches the message Jesus taught. Jesus continues to disclose some interesting thoughts in **Verse 17**.

17 For verily I say unto you, That many prophets and righteous *men* have desired to see *those things* which ye see and have not seen *them;* and to hear *those things* which ye hear and have not heard *them.*

> **17** There were many prophets (interpreters who reveal the hidden oracles, God's spokesman) and upright, virtuous men, who keep the commandments that desired and longed to see the times of the Messiah that had been prophesied and proclaimed through the ages yet never saw what you now see happening before you, they never heard in their presence what you are now hearing. (DHP)

The Old Testament prophets and righteous men did not see or hear what? The revealing of the mysteries of the Kingdom that His disciples were experiencing firsthand. At best, they only knew about them in types and shadows of what was to come.

Another side note:

Luke 16:16

16 The law and the prophets *were* until John: since that time the kingdom of God is preached, and every man presseth into it.

16 The law and the prophets remained until John, since then, the good news about the Kingdom of God has been proclaimed, and everyone entering it is under attack. (International Standard Version)

The Pentateuch (Genesis-Deuteronomy) revealed the law, then Joshua through Malachi, the major and minor prophets referenced the coming of a king and his kingdom. These all heard and even proclaimed of a coming king and his kingdom, but never saw or experienced what Jesus disciples and you and I have heard, seen, and experienced. I find it compelling that the International Standard Version of **Verse 16** says, "everyone entering it is under attack."

In my 49 years of ministry (at the release of this book, Spring 2024), never had I experienced first-hand the hatred, attacks, the loss of what I thought were covenant relationships until I heard, received, believed on, and then began to preach this kingdom message. In Luke's gospel, Jesus states that the message of the law and a coming kingdom through the prophets was preached until John (the Baptist). Wait!!! Until John, then He said that the message would change. Why? Because He, Jesus had come to fulfill the law since man could not, then reveal the Father's plan of the king, His kingdom, and their purpose. This messages greatest enemy is religion and the self-imposed traditions of men.

So, I continue to proclaim **many preach messages about Jesus,** but **not many preach the message Jesus preached**.

One more scriptural proof of preaching this message will bring attacks, from religious men often influenced by the "messenger of Satan." The Apostle Paul was harassed because of the messenger he carried and preached fulfilling his kingdom assignment.

2 Corinthians 12:7-10

7 And lest I should be exalted above measure through the abundance of the revelations, there was given to me a thorn in the flesh, the messenger of Satan to buffet me, lest I should be exalted above measure.

> **7** The thorn (the troublesome and painful trials, the attacks) which satan (the adversary of the King and his kingdom) continually brought against me was actually a gift, reminding me to not revert back to the prideful, arrogant man that I once was. It kept me from becoming haughty and self-exalted thinking the extraordinary events and revelations (manifestations, appearances, experiencing the third realm of heaven, being taught by Christ himself) that I received from the Lord would cause to me to have preeminence over those he called me to. (DHP)

An interesting side note on the phrase, "a thorn in the flesh." The Greek word for **thorn** is not found another time in the entire New Testament.

8 For this thing I besought the Lord thrice, that it might depart from me.

> **8** Because of these on-going trials and attacks, I earnestly sought the Lord three different times that they would be withdrawn and desist. (DHP)

9 And he said unto me, My grace is sufficient for thee: for my strength is made perfect in weakness. Most gladly therefore will I rather glory in my infirmities, that the power of Christ may rest upon me.

> **9** Each time, the Lord's response was the same, "your life is now governed by the power of my divine grace which enables you (gives you the authority to act) to do the things I have revealed and imparted unto you. My strength, power, and ability will carry you through your time of weakness, frailty, and when your strength is fading." Then I understood that his presence, the truths that he has imparted to me are more than any compensation that I could receive, it is his strength in me, not that of my own that reveals the Christ. (DHP)

10 Therefore I take pleasure in infirmities, in reproaches, in necessities, in persecutions, in distresses for Christ's sake: for when I am weak, then am I strong.

> **10** I rejoice, I count it a privilege to go through the things that I have and will, injury, distress, persecution and calamities for Christ's cause and purpose being fulfilled in my life, it is then when his strength is once again imparted to me and overrides my weakness, enabling me to bear up under and overcome them. (DHP)

Because of the depth of information that we are pursuing, we will continue these thoughts in the next chapter (7).

CHAPTER SEVEN
THE PARABLE OF THE SOWER (PART 2)

As we continue looking into the kingdom parable that Jesus taught in **Matthew 13**, let us closely inspect the next several verses (**Verses 18-23**) in His teaching, Jesus began to explain (expand) the Parable of the Sower to His disciples after they questioned His reasoning for teaching in Parables.

Matthew 13:18-19

18 Hear ye therefore the parable of the sower.

> 18 Give ear to this teaching, comprehend (grasp, embrace it) until you understand the spiritual meaning of this earthly story dealing with the Sower, the seed, the soil, and the potential fruit. (DHP)

19 When any one heareth the word of the kingdom, and understandeth *it* not, then cometh the wicked *one,* and catcheth

away that which was sown in his heart. This is he which received seed by the wayside.

> **19** If you only hear, but do not comprehend the doctrine and precepts explained in this kingdom key, the enemy of these truths, satan (the evil one) makes his appearance to try to influence your thoughts against these principles, then, if he succeeds, he seizes (takes by force) the seed the Sower released, removing it from the heart (soil, mind), this soil has become so beaten down that a plow hasn't touched it, so the soil has not depth, thus making it easy for the enemy to steal the exposed seed. (DHP)

In John Gill's commentary, his notes on the phrase, "and understandeth it not" are extremely insightful:

"and understandeth it not with his heart. He is one that is careless and inattentive, negligent and forgetful; has some slight notions of things as he hears, but these pass away as they come; his affections are not at all touched, nor his judgment informed by them, but remains as stupid, and as unconcerned as ever; his heart is not opened to attend to, and receive the word, but continues hard and obdurate; and is like the common and beaten road, that is trodden down by everyone, and is not susceptible of the seed, that falls upon it." (John Gill)

"perhaps more properly, regardeth it not, does not lay his heart to it" (Adam Clarke)

When Jesus said, "and understandeth it not," what was he referencing? The answer is found in the first few words in **Verse 19**, "the word of the kingdom."

The word **understandeth** is the Greek word *"suniemi"* (pronounced: soon-ee-ay-mee) which references, "perceiving, to set or join together in mind."

At this point, once again he expounds to his disciples what He had shared with the multitude, emphasizing the soil types. January 2024 will begin my forty-ninth year of ministry, having pioneered several churches, extensively traveling this nation and other parts of the world. I have come to realize something very important. All too often, people attending their local churches, attending conferences, revivals, and camp meetings are quick to blame the messenger, even the message, as to the lack of results in their life, the lack of evident fruit the leader spoke of, and the absence of kingdom benefits taught.

Seldom do they look internally, questioning the type or condition of their own soil (mind, heart) being the hindrance. In Jesus exhortation of this kingdom parable of the Sower, the seed, and the soil, he associates the lack of production (the harvest of the seed sown) on the condition of the soil, **NOT** the Sower or the seed.

On any given corporate service, the potential is there for all four soils to be in the service. The following mathematical example may not be too popular but here goes, doing the math, if all four soils are in a service in equal portions, only about 25% of the congregations' soil is conducive to the 100-fold increase spoken of by Jesus in **Matthew 13:8**.

We will look more in-depth at the four different types of soil later in this book, but for now, here are the soil types and the scriptures where they are revealed:

1. **The Wayside Soil (Matthew 13:4,19)**
2. **The Stony Place Soil (Matthew 13:5,20-21)**
3. **The Thorny Soil (Matthew 13:7,22)**
4. **The Good Ground Soil (Matthew 13:8,23)**

I believe one of the biggest hindrances to the seeds potential return can be found in an often quoted, but seldom understood verse of scripture also in Matthew's gospel. God did not leave us in the dark as to what is important and a must priority for our lives. **He wants his priority to be our priority! The Kingdom must be first, everything else is second.**

Dr. Munroe once made this statement, "nothing is yours until you understand it."[1] To walk in the kingdom, to use its keys, you first must come to an understanding of it through your pursuit and your study until it becomes a rhema revelation to you, then you can/will enjoy all its benefits.

Matthew 6:33

33 But seek ye first the kingdom of God, and his righteousness; and all these things shall be added unto you.

> 33 First (in rank, influence, the chief or principal thing) pursue, search for/out, chase down, put your whole heart into God's kingdom (his dominion, power, rule), make it of the upmost importance, first in your thoughts and actions, become established in his righteousness, this brings you into God's approval, this gives you entrance into his kingdom and glory, then all the things that I have spoken to you (**Verses 25-34**), the earthly things will be added to you since you put the heavenly things first. (DHP)

Synonyms for the word **seek** are "pursue, investigate, explore, learn, go after, understand, consider, and desire." The Greek word **first** is "*proton*" which means, "first in time, place, rank, influence, honor, the chief or principal thing." In the simplest definition, "**first things first**."

Starting back in **Verse 25**, Jesus said, "**take no thought.**" If you read these verses in context all the way down into **Verse 34**, I believe what He was saying, and it is confirmed in the Greek translation of the phrase was, "these things should not consume your thoughts, feelings, emotions, time, or energy. These can be distractions to your purpose, calling, and destiny. Avoid any distraction that hinders your purpose.

The Greek word that makes up the phrase "**take no thought**" is "*merimnao*" (pronounced: mer-im-nah-o) and defines as, "do not be anxious, concern yourself with, occupy your thoughts with, or trouble yourself with cares." Another derivative of the word states, "through the idea of distraction."

Jesus then uses the analogy of being preoccupied and it results in **Verse 27**.

Matthew 6:27

27 Which of you by taking thought can add one cubit unto his stature?

> **27** No amount of thought, being anxious, or troubling yourself can change your height or age, those thoughts will not add one inch to your height or one year to your age. (DHP)

In **Verses 31-32**, He explains in more detail these distractions:

31 Therefore take no thought, saying, What shall we eat? or, What shall we drink? or, Wherewithal shall we be clothed?

> **31** Consequently, do not allow your thoughts to consume you to the point that your language takes on what you think saying, "what are we going to eat, drink, or wear?" (DHP)

In John Gill's commentary, he states that these repetitive expressions reveal a man of little faith.

32 (For after all these things do the Gentiles seek:) for your heavenly Father knoweth that ye have need of all these things.

> **32** These are the things the world spends all of its time and energy craving, demanding, and clamoring for, but my father and yours understands the needs of his children, why? He is our father; he knows the needs we have daily. (DHP)

Another thought as we continue: The enemy will increase his attacks when he knows you are getting close/closer to the answer, when the light is being turned on and your life is about to be forever changed. He also attacks those who sow these kingdom principles (seeds) into people, individually and corporately. This message must become a revelation, a rhema word to you. Do not try to operate in them until they are rooted and grounded in the correct soil,. Allow Holy Spirit to reveal your present soil, then, allow Him to do His work in you to produce the right, productive soil. This will stop much heartache, disappointment, and discouragement.

There is a huge difference as we have referenced in this manuscript between "**hearing**" and "**knowing**." Hearing a truth without it taking root, developing, and maturing in the proper soil and folks trying to act on/apply it will cause damage to yourself and potentially others.

Let us look at this example in the scriptures:

Acts 19:8-16

8 And he went into the synagogue, and spake boldly for the space of three months, disputing and persuading the things concerning the kingdom of God.

9 But when divers were hardened, and believed not, but spake evil of that way before the multitude, he departed from them, and separated the disciples, disputing daily in the school of one Tyrannus.

10 And this continued by the space of two years; so that all they which dwelt in Asia heard the word of the Lord Jesus, both Jews and Greeks.

11 And God wrought special miracles by the hands of Paul:

12 So that from his body were brought unto the sick handkerchiefs or aprons, and the diseases departed from them, and the evil spirits went out of them.

13 Then certain of the vagabond Jews, exorcists, took upon them to call over them which had evil spirits the name of the Lord Jesus, saying, We adjure you by Jesus whom Paul preacheth.

14 And there were seven sons of *one* Sceva, a Jew, *and* chief of the priests, which did so.

15 And the evil spirit answered and said, Jesus I know, and Paul I know; but who are ye?

16 And the man in whom the evil spirit was leaped on them, and overcame them, and prevailed against them, so that they fled out of that house naked and wounded.

THERE ARE A FEW THINGS IN THE ABOVE PASSAGE OF SCRIPTURE that should be examined in light of what I wrote in the paragraphs preceding it.

- The Apostle Paul taught for three months in the synagogue in Ephesus (**Verse 8**). The King James uses the words "disputing" and "persuading." What did he teach? The Kingdom! The word **disputing** is the Greek word "*dialegomai*" (pronounced: dee-al-eg-om-ahee), and it translates as, "to discourse with, to converse, to discuss." The other definition that grabbed my attention was this, "to think different within one's self, to mingle thought with thought." Paul was conversing with some disciples and people in the church in Ephesus, he was teaching the kingdom, which by the word **disputing's** meaning, was challenging them that they would have to think differently than they had thought in order to see and experience the kingdom. Then we have the word, **persuading**. It is the Greek word, "*peitho*" (pronounced: pi-tho) which defines as, "to induce one by words to believe, to convince." He was challenging their beliefs with the message of the kingdom, He was stating that their thoughts would have to change to see, understand, and experience the revelation he was endeavoring to impart. Remember, "For as he thinketh in his heart, so is he…" (**Proverbs 23:7**) The word **heart** also translates as **soul,** which throughout this manuscript I have interchanged with the word **soil**. As your soul (soil) gives thought to the seed being sown, depending on the condition of your soil and which of the four types it is, dictates the rejection of the seed, the return from the seed, or the lack thereof.

- Upon hearing the kingdom message, some became very obstinate, unyielding to the message, refusing to believe the truths Paul was revealing (I have often taught that unbelief is far more dangerous than doubt, as doubt is a lack of information, but unbelief is a decision. You cannot operate in unbelief until after you have heard, then reject it). Those that rejected it immediately tried to impact others addressing the messenger and the message with offensive language. Remember: In **Matthew 13**, the kingdom parable states how quickly the enemy comes to steal the seed (message) before it can take root, and sadly, often, he uses religious unlearned people. Paul took the disciples (he separated the wheat from the tares) into the school Tyrannus and continued to teach them. (**Verse 9**)

John Gill in his commentary on the phrase, "**he departed from them**" wrote this, "the hardened, unbelieving, and blaspheming Jews, as being unworthy of the means of grace; he went out of their synagogue, and no more entered there: and separated the disciples; from them, the twelve disciples he had laid his hands on, and others who in this space of time, the space of three months, had been converted under his ministry; these he formed into a separate Gospel church state, as well as engaged them to quit the company and conversation of these blasphemers, and no more attend with them in their synagogue, that so they might not be infected and corrupted by them; a separation from such who contradict and blaspheme the truths and ordinances of the Gospel, is justifiable."

- Paul stayed in Asia and Ephesus, the chief city in Asia, for two years teaching and training, until all of that region of Asia had heard the kingdom message. If you are a minister reading this, do not let opposition, or religious mindsets sidetrack your purpose or your message. Your purpose is to preach/teach the message, the message is the kingdom! (**Verse 10**)

- Jesus preached the kingdom for 3.5 years and countless, signs, wonders, and miracles accompanied His message. Preaching the right message brings the right manifestations, they are confirmations, confirming the message with signs following. The Apostle Paul continues Jesus's message and look what happens: Paul's teaching produced remarkable, uncommon, unusual miracles, even to the point that **handkerchiefs** (Greek word "*soudarion*" pronounced: soo-dar-ee-on, meaning a cloth for wiping the perspiration from the face, a sweat cloth) and aprons (a linen covering that workman and servants were accustomed to wearing) taken from Paul which he used/wore and placed them on the sick and possessed, the sick were healed and the possessed were delivered. (**Verses 11-12**)

Once again, the notes in John Gill's Commentary shed more light on this: "**So that from his body were brought unto the sick.**" The Ethiopic version renders it, "from the extremity", or "border of his garment"; and the Syriac version, "from the garments which were upon his body"; were brought and put upon the sick; that is, of the clothes which the apostle wore, some of them were taken and carried to sick persons, and used by them: particularly "handkerchiefs" or "aprons"; the former were such as he might use to wipe his face with, and remove sweat, or any filth from the body; and the latter, what he might wear as a mechanic, when working at his trade:

- The Seven Sons of Sceva. During that time there were a group of wandering self-proclaimed exorcists, professing to tell people's fortunes, claiming to cure diseases with charms and spells. Hummm, I wonder if they were a group of uncommitted, unsubmitted, back-slidden prophets…just a thought. Sceva (means "mind reader") was a certain chief priest in Ephesus who had seven sons that were the wandering group following in his footsteps.

Apparently, they heard Paul speak to and cast out spirits, so they took it upon themselves to attempt to operate in a kingdom key based on a phrase they heard Paul use, and a Name they had no understanding of or relationship with. "We restrain you in the name that Paul preaches (proclaims)." And what happened? Wait for it…the evil spirit said,

"I know Jesus is the Son of God, I know he has the power to dispossess (deprive to stay) spirits, and Paul, I am acquainted with him being a servant of the most high God, but who or what are you? You definitely are not a disciple of Jesus nor a servant of God, but you are children of the devil, you have no power over us, but on the other hand, you are subject to us." (DHP)

What was the result? The evil spirit through the possessed man grabbed a hold of them, beat them, wounded them, and stripped them naked. **(Verses 13-16)**

- What was the result? The reverence of God hit Ephesus and Asia, Jesus was exalted and celebrated, true repentance swept the countryside, conviction caused them to act bringing their books which they used for magic, soothsaying, necromancy, conjuring spirits and burned them in front of all in Ephesus, which was worth an incredible amount of money. In the end the Word of God increased in the region and overcame everything. **(Verses 17-20)**

---

1. Munroe, Myles. "Nothing if Yours Until You Understand It." YouTube video, 0:15. February 24, 2022. https://www.youtube.com/shorts/ 2Q8yo2_9AsA.

THE FOUR SOIL TYPES

CHAPTER EIGHT
THE WAY-SIDE SOIL

ALL TOO OFTEN IN CHURCHES ON SUNDAY MORNINGS, MANY IN the congregation will critique (assess, evaluate) the minister and their message through the lens of their own perception, life, present situations, or even their past, Yet I find it extremely interesting in this kingdom parable in **Matthew 13**, the Sower (minister) assesses the soil in those he is sowing into.

Matthew 13:4,19

4 He released (sowed) the seed and as it descended, it first landed upon a ground that the plow had not touched, so, because of the soil's hardened (unplowed) condition, the opportunity to sink into the earth was not there, then the seed laying exposed in the open made easy access to the fowls (the seed's enemy) to make its appearance, devour, consume, and eat the seed not meant for it. (DHP)

19 If you only hear, but do not comprehend the doctrine and precepts explained in this kingdom key, the enemy of these truths, satan (the evil one) makes his appearance to try to influence your thoughts against these principles, then, if he succeeds, he seizes (takes by force) the seed the Sower released, removing it from the heart (soil, mind), this soil has become so beaten down that a plow hasn't touched it, so the soil has not depth, thus making it easy for the enemy to steal the exposed seed. (DHP)

The KJV uses the phrase in **Verses 4,19** to describe the first type of soil as, **"way side**." Way-side soil sketches the idea of a hard beaten path in which no plow had broken up the ground, so there was no real opportunity for the seed to sink into, then take root in the soil. This also represents a ground trampled on by men, then because of no real depth and openness as a plow had not touched it, the seed was easily exposed and because clearly accessible prey to the fowls of the air.

The concept of a "hard beaten path" communicates its present condition was something that had developed over time. I want to challenge you to consider some thoughts prophetically concerning this first type of soil. This hardened soil was the reason that the seed did not take root, develop, and grow.

———

LET'S DELVE INTO SOME TRUTHS REFERENCING THESE FOUR different soils, as I am convinced recognizing which soil we have, and why, with the Holy Spirit's help will reveal which soil it is, remove the things that have produced the wrong type of soil, heal us, and change our soil to good fertile ground that will produce the 100-fold return on the seed as promised.

One of the above references states that the path had hardened because the plow had not been applied. One reference stated the "way side" soil could also represent private paths that the individual had taken (almost presenting the concept that these were areas no one was allowed to see or walk them through…my thoughts).

As a result of the soil's condition, people had trampled on this person's soil (mind) greatly hindering the potential outcome. So, in this individual's life, the seed was never correctly planted which gave easy access to be devoured by the seed's greatest enemy (satan).

This soil can also speak of a hearer that is inattentive, negligent, then because of their negligence, correct, proper understanding does not happen so their judgment is off, their affection (love) for the seed (word) wanes. This person is distracted (even in corporate worship), preoccupied (mostly with the cares of life, things that have no eternal outcome, or things that have nothing to do with the service), eventually becoming skeptical of the Sower (minister) and the message (seed). They are not those who readily receive God's Word. Look again at **James 1:21**.

21 Wherefore lay apart all filthiness and superfluity of naughtiness, and receive with meekness the engrafted word, which is able to save your souls.

> **21** On account of this, put away (lay down) everything that is defiled, dishonorable, morally wicked, any/all residue that has tried to remain prior to your conversion in Christ. Embrace

(take a hold of) with a genuine humility the nature and seed of Christ (his word) which has been planted in you, allow it to germinate, grow, sprout up and produce, in doing this, you will deliver your mind, will, and emotions from the former things and reveal good soil, ready for harvest. (DHP)

John Gill states in his commentary, **"and the fowls came and devoured them**." The other evangelists say, "the fowls of the air." The Vulgate Latin and Munster's Hebrew Gospel, and some copies; and mean the devils; so called, because their habitation is in the air; hence they are said to be "the power of the air": and because of their ravenous and devouring nature, their swiftness to do mischief, and their flocking in multitudes, where the word is preached, to hinder its usefulness, as fowls do, where seed is sowing. Satan, and his principalities, and powers, rove about in the air, come down on earth, and seek whom they may devour, and often mix themselves in religious assemblies, to do what mischief they can; see **Job 1:6**.[1] "Now there was a day when the sons of God came to present themselves before the LORD, and Satan came also among them."

Another reason for the wayside soil (hard beaten path) was that a plow had not touched it. I want to challenge us right here to think "outside of the box" for a moment.

Hosea 10:11b-12

11b "...**Judah shall plow**, *and* Jacob shall break his clods."

    11b "praise (Judah) plows." (DHP)

12 Sow to yourselves in righteousness, reap in mercy; break up your fallow ground: for *it is* time to seek the LORD, till he come and rain righteousness upon you.

> **12** Sow (plant), become pregnant, then yield/produce because of our right standing with him based on his righteousness, your harvest will be the result of his mercy, this will happen when you freshly till the ground that was untilled (this is our responsibility), worship (Hebrew word, "*darash*" pronounced, daw-rash) until the rain comes (this also will moisten the ground in preparation for the seed that is to be sown), the rain is a sign of our right standing with him and our worship of him. (DHP)

This truth is again revealed in the book of **Zechariah 14:17**:

17 And it shall be, that whoso will not come up of all the families of the earth unto Jerusalem to worship the King, the LORD of hosts, even upon them shall be no rain.

The equation is quite simple: No worship=No rain=No crops/harvest. Selah!

Judah is the Hebrew word "*Yehudah*" (pronounced: yeh-hoo-daw) which means, "praise." The phrase, "**break up the fallow ground**" is the Hebrew word, "*niyr*" (pronounced: neer) which translates as, "to freshly plow, to till."

The writer of Judges (some traditional views believe that the Prophet Samuel wrote it) makes these prophetic statements in his writings. After Joshua's death, Israel asks the Lord who was to go into battle against the Canaanites? The Lord answered with, "Judah shall go up." **Up** is the Hebrew word, "*alah*" (pronounced: aw-law) and defines as, "to ascend up, to mount up, to come up (before God). Praise takes you to a higher realm, it brings you up into/before the presence of God.

Judges 1:1-2

1 Now after the death of Joshua it came to pass, that the children of Israel asked the LORD, saying, Who shall go up for us against the Canaanites first, to fight against them?

2 And the LORD said, **Judah shall go up**: behold, I have delivered the land into his hand.

This type of praise and worship before God will assure you of the conquest in the battles of life that you are facing. Once again, Israel asks who was to go up first in battle against Benjamin. The answer was the same.

Judges 20:18

18 And the children of Israel arose, and went up to the house of God, and asked counsel of God, and said, Which of us shall go up first to the battle against the children of Benjamin? And the LORD said, **Judah shall go up first**.

Another interesting and I believe very revealing prophetic truth. Which one of the twelve tribes of Israel that were encamped around the tabernacle of Moses (the pattern that he built according to God's blueprints, where his presence would tabernacle among His people) had direct immediate access into the door (the east entrance) of God's presence?

Numbers 2:3

3 And on the east side toward the rising of the sun shall they of the standard of the camp of **Judah** pitch throughout their armies:

and Nahshon the son of Amminadab shall be captain of the children of **Judah**.

Judah was camped directly in front of the east entrance of the Tabernacle. Also, that was the only entrance into it. Can you begin to see the prophetic significance? Praise and worship will bring you into the Father's presence. Why does the majority of the Ekklesia (church) start their corporate services with praise and worship? Because it is groundbreaking, it plows, tills, loosens the soil (mind, heart), it also removes anything that may have gotten into the soil (the mind during the week that could hinder), preparing it to receive the seed.

What are we allowing that keeps us from worshipping (preparing) our soil for the promised benefits and harvest in the scriptures? We will look into and reveal the answer in the rest of this chapter.

Matthew 13:15

15 For the **hearts of these people are hardened**, and their ears cannot hear, and they have closed their eyes- so their eyes cannot see, and their ears cannot hear, and their hearts cannot understand, and they cannot turn to me and let me heal them. (NLT)

Mark 6:52

52 For they considered not *the miracle* of the loaves: **for their heart was hardened**.

Mark 16:14

14 Afterward he appeared unto the eleven as they sat at meat, and upbraided them with **their unbelief and hardness of heart**, because they believed not them which had seen him after he was risen.

Remember, a hard heart is often the result of unbelief, which is a decision, a choice, after you have heard or seen, then rejected it.

Romans 8:7

7 Because the carnal mind *is* enmity against God: for it is not subject to the law of God, neither indeed can be.

> 7 The carnal mind (one whose dictates come from their flesh) whose decisions and actions are external (not from the Spirit/heart), the physical sensuous nature which the wisdom of God does not flow though, but on the contrary, it is the complete opposite, it is in opposition towards God. The fleshly mind will not operate by the commands and precepts of God stated throughout his word, that mindset is unable to see, let alone walk in them because of its own rebellion. (DHP)

Jeremiah, the prophet penned these very strong words:

Jeremiah 17:9

9 The heart *is* deceitful above all *things,* and desperately wicked: who can know it?

Some of the better definitions of the Hebrew word **heart** (from Strong's and Brown-Driver-Biggs) refers to the mind, will, and soul, the seat of man's appetites. The derivative of the Hebrew word #H6117 describes someone being tripped up around their heels. I know you are not necessarily supposed to do this when writing a book (but since it is mine...lol), WOW!!! When our mind and will are operating out of deception, we are the cause of being tripped up, the falls, and mistakes.

I feel this so strongly as I am writing the final thoughts of this chapter, I want to pray this prayer for myself and all those who will pray it with me (out loud) as you read it and it quickens something inside of us, even convicting us.

————

Father, we come to you in a true heart of repentance, forgive us for allowing the cares of this world and life to override the very principles you have spoken to us through your word. Today, right now, we choose, we purpose to once again become a people that understands your purpose for creating (forming) us was for your glory, and for your praise (**Isaiah 43:7,21**). This is the day that the true worshippers are rising up and fulfilling **John 4:23**, we desire to be those who worship you from the heart, in the right spirit and truth. No longer will we allow distractions, old mindsets, feelings, or emotions to steal our praise, our soil will be rich and prepared through our worship to receive your incorruptible seed (your kingdom message from your kingdom messenger). Our fruit will no longer be hindered, prolonged, or stopped because our heart, soil, and mind are right, then, coupled together with our praise, we will receive the 100-fold return as you declared in your Kingdom parable in **Matthew 13**. In the powerful, matchless name of Jesus, the Christ, Amen, and Amen.

———————

1. John Gill, *Exposition of the Entire Bible* (published 1748-1763, 1809), accessed from e-Sword Online Bible, public domain.

CHAPTER NINE
THE STONY GROUND

MATTHEW 13:5,6, 20,21

5 Some fell upon **stony places**, where they had not much earth: and forthwith they sprung up, because they had no deepness of earth:

> **5** Some of the seed sown fell upon rocky places (where there was more rock than soil), where there was little earth, the rocks were in such mass that the roots that would be produced from the seed could not go down into the soil (earth) where there would be enough moisture to support the potential plant, so almost immediately, the exposed seed shot up a sprout because the soil lacked any depth. (DHP)

Other meanings of the words, "stony places" are shallow, immature, carnal. I believe this type of soil also represents those who walk in and are easily offended. The sad part is, often many are swift to look at and judge others so quickly, but never truly look within to see the things that cause offense within themselves. Here is a verse that all of us should strive to develop and walk in:

Psalm 119:165

165 Great peace have they which love thy law: and nothing shall offend them.

> **165** Those who truly love God's instruction and teachings, nothing will steal their peace, cause a stumbling block or fall into offense. (DHP)

The Apostle Peter confirms these thoughts in his writings:

1 Peter 2:6-8

6 Wherefore also it is contained in the scripture, Behold, I lay in Sion a chief corner stone, elect, precious: and he that believeth on him shall not be confounded.

7 Unto you therefore which believe *he is* precious: but unto them which be disobedient, the stone which the builders disallowed, the same is made the head of the corner,

8 And a stone of stumbling, and a rock of offence, *even to them* which stumble at the word, being disobedient: whereunto also they were appointed.

Peter affirms that Christ is the "chief corner stone" which is the first stone (rock) that is placed once the foundation is laid by the Apostles and Prophets (**See Ephesians 2:20**). Those who are disobedient to the revelation, those who reject the truths he taught cause their own stumbling which they then become offended at by rejecting them. I call it self-deception.

Earlier in Peter's life, he is the one that received and the first to declare that Jesus was the Christ. Once he proclaimed it, Jesus said to him, "...upon this rock I will build My church..." (**See Mathew 16:18-19**). Christ is the Chief Cornerstone (the rock), the message of Christ and the Kingdom (which was the message he preached), and that is a key given to Peter and now us to continue his message.

Often in those with this type of soil, there is a quick response, but because of the shallowness of the soil, it does not grow a deep root base. Charles Spurgeon once said, "some folks seen to have been baptized in boiling water, requiring constant superficial excitement to remain in the faith. When trouble and persecution come, they leave quickly. Their idea of discipleship has no place for suffering, they are fair-weather Christians."[1]

———

MY GUESS IS THESE TYPES OF INDIVIDUALS HAVE NEVER HEARD or were taught **1 Peter 5:10**:

10 But the God of all grace, who hath called us unto his eternal glory by Christ Jesus, after that ye have suffered a while, make you perfect, stablish, strengthen, settle you. (KJV)

10 After you have suffered for a little while, the God of all grace [who imparts His blessing and favor], who called you to His *own* eternal glory in Christ, will Himself complete, confirm, strengthen, and establish you [making you what you ought to be]. (The Amplified Bible)

10 And then, after your brief suffering, the God of all loving grace, who has called you to share in his eternal glory in Christ, will personally and powerfully restore you and make you stronger than ever. Yes, he will set you firmly in place and build you up. (TPT)

> **10** God who is rich in grace, loving kindness, and mercy has summoned us to participate in all that his glory reveals which is perpetual, eternal, forever, which has no end, which is ours through Christ as he is "**in us**" and we are "**in him**." You will experience some affliction, difficulties, distress and hardship for a little while (short seasons), these things are not meant to destroy or punish you, but to strengthen you and your beliefs, to equip you, to prepare you to walk in all that I have called you to, you will be become immoveable, strong with spiritual power and knowledge, all because your foundation is firm, solid, and can not be shaken. (DHP)

Endurance is seldom taught let alone acted upon. However, there are promises to those who endure. **Matthew 24:13-14** says:

13 But he that shall endure unto the end, the same shall be saved.

> **13** Those who continue to stand during affliction, trials, and persecution, especially because of their faith, at the end of all of this, they will be found safe and sound, rescued from all danger and destruction. (DHP)

14 And this gospel of the kingdom shall be preached in all the world for a witness unto all nations; and then shall the end come.

14 The message of the kingdom (God's rule and reign, dominion, and power) will be proclaimed, heralded, and published throughout the whole world with evidence (proof, confirmation) supporting the facts that this is the right message because of the right manifestations, not until then will there be a consummation of all things. (DHP)

————

THE JEWS REFERRED TO THESE STONY PLACES AS BARREN, A place not fit for sowing. John Gill's notes in his commentary of **Verse 5** are a little lengthy, however well worth the read so I added them here.

"And forthwith they sprung up, because they had no deepness of earth"; to strike their roots downwards: and through the reflection of the heat, upon the rocks and stones, they quickly broke through the thin surface of the earth over them, and appeared above ground before the usual time of the springing up of seed: which may not only denote the immediate reception of the word by these hearers, and their quick assent to it; but their sudden and hasty profession of it, without taking due time to consider the nature and importance thereof; and the seeming cheerfulness in which they did both receive and profess it; though it was only outward and hypocritical, and more on account of the manner of preaching it, than the word itself, and through a selfish principle in them; and did not arise from any real experience of the power of it on their souls, or true spiritual pleasure in it: nor could it be otherwise, since their stony hearts were not taken away, nor hearts of flesh given them; wherefore the word had no place in them, and made no real impression on them; they remained dead in trespasses and sins; the word was not the savour of life unto life unto them, or the Spirit that giveth life; they did not become living and lively stones; they continued as insensible as ever of their state and condition by nature, of the exceeding sinfulness of sin, of the danger they were in, and of their need of Christ, and salvation by him; they were as hard, and obdurate, and as inflexible, as ever, without any real contrition for sin, or meltings of soul through the influence of the love and grace of God; and as backward as ever to submit to the righteousness of Christ, being stout hearted, and far from it; and being no more cordially willing to be subject to the sceptre of his kingdom, or to serve him in righteousness and holiness, than they ever were; for the word falling upon them, made no change in them; their hearts were as hard as ever, notwithstanding the seeming and hasty reception of it; though they did not refuse to hearken to the word externally, did not put away the shoulder, or stop their ears, yet their hearts were still like an adamant stone: nothing but the mighty power of God, and his efficacious grace, can break the rocky heart in pieces; or give an heart of flesh, a sensible, soft, and flexible one, with which a man truly repents of sin, believes in Christ, and becomes subject to him.

---

6 AND WHEN THE SUN WAS UP, THEY WERE SCORCHED; AND because they had no root, they withered away.

> **6** Then, when things get hot, when the heat is turned up, then because the seed has no covering, when difficulty, trials, or tragedy arrive, the seed's potential is wasted. (DHP)

20 But he that received the seed into stony places, the same is he that heareth the word, and anon (at once, immediately) with joy receiveth it;

> **20** Those whose soil is full of rocks, whose hearts are hardened, who refuse to allow the seed (word) break them, so they continue a life without true repentance, having only a form of godliness, this person will initially give quick audience to the word (seed) that is being sown, and even show some level of external rejoicing. (DHP)

Albert Barnes wrote, **"But he that received the seed into stony places."** - Jesus explains this as denoting those who hear the gospel; who are caught with it as something new or pleasing; who profess to be greatly delighted with it, and who are full of zeal for it. Yet they have no root in themselves. They are not true Christians. Their hearts are not changed. They have not seen their guilt and danger, and the true excellency of Christ. They are not "really" attached to the gospel; and when they are tried and persecution comes, they fall - as the rootless grain withers before the scorching rays of the noonday sun. (Albert Barnes Commentary)

21 Yet hath he not root in himself, but dureth for a while: for when tribulation or persecution ariseth because of the word, by and by he is offended.

21 Shortly after he hears it, troubles and persecutions come because of the kingdom message he received. Then he quickly falls away, for the truth did not sink deeply into his heart. (**TPT**)

The Passion Translation states that this individual heard the "kingdom message" but almost immediately trouble and persecution came. Why? Not because of the person, but the potential the seed (message) carried. Why does he turn away? I believe he turned away having no insight, revelation, or illumination as to why the trouble and persecution came. Him taking **offense** (see **Verse 21** in the KJV above) so quickly in his soil (mind) stopped the seed's process, not allowing it into the innermost parts of his being.

The New American Standard Version says, "he has no firm root in himself."

The Amplified says, "he has no substantial root in himself."

Here is another thought to consider, he was never truly rooted and grounded in the "In Christ" realities to begin with. It may look like his soil (soul, mind) is deep, prepared, even fertile, but the rock, the hardness of heart, the offense, all the things to hinder the seed lay right under the shallow soil.

The phrase "hath not root in himself" really describes someone who has no depth of the seed (the Word of God) in them, possibly just enough to look the part, but not any depth to sustain him or his beliefs and actions when the persecution and trouble come.

> **21** The seed never fully develops as the soil is so shallow that the roots can't grow deep, thus his endurance is limited, minimal, and weak, so, when the pressure increases, when trouble and persecution come because of what the seed (message) is carrying and can manifest, immediately his immaturity is exposed because he has no real confidence and

trust in God, now he is offended at the messenger and the message and is tripped up and stumbles (falls). (DHP)

This type of individual is typical of many that believe in and profess Jesus to be their savior, but have yet to experience Him as Lord. They entered the door (which is Christ), but have remained in the outer court, only hearing a sin-conscious message, yet because of the type of church they attend, what their doctrines and beliefs are, and the message they have sat under, have never come into the revelation that there were three rooms in the Tabernacle of Moses, which was a type and shadow of what was to come, the Tabernacle of Jesus. They have not been taught that Jesus lives in a three-room house, you come in the outer court at the New Birth, then you move in Pentecost, the Holy Place and finally sonship, a mature son, the Holy of Holies where all the attributes of God are made manifest through His many-membered Christ (the mature sons) in the earth.

———

A FEW FINAL THOUGHTS AS WE CLOSE OUT THIS CHAPTER. Excitement, shouting, running around the building, or even falling out in the presence of God is not the proof that the seed took, as all of us who have lived a while on this earth know and can relate. It has everything to do with the soil, the heart, and the mind. Selah!

The Stony ground because of the shallowness of its soil, with more rocks under the surface than the soil that can be seen on the surface speaks of never really being fully connected or fastened to the message of the kingdom. Even though the seed (message) was preached (sown), the seed never rooted, so the heat of the persecution singed the seed, stopped its growth, and no plant or fruit was produced.

---

1. The information referenced in this work is attributed to 'Morning and Evening' by Charles Spurgeon, accessed from the Christian Classics Ethereal Library (CCEL) at https://ccel.org/ccel/spurgeon/sermons49/sermons49.xxxv.html. The Christian Classics Ethereal Library is an online resource that provides access to classic Christian literature and is not affiliated with the author or publisher of this work."

CHAPTER TEN
THE THORNY GROUND

MATTHEW 13:7,22

7 And some fell among thorns; and the thorns sprung up, and choked them:

> 7 Some seed fell on the ground filled with briars (shrubs full of thorns) and because this field had not been completely or properly cleared, the thorns and briars remained. (DHP)

Because the thorns still remained, the freshly sown seed was negatively impacted as the thorns choked the seeds potential.

"They grew with the grain, crowded it, shaded it, exhausted the earth, and thus choked it." (Albert Barnes Commentary)

22 He also that received seed among the thorns is he that heareth the word; and the care of this world, and the deceitfulness of riches, choke the word, and he becometh unfruitful.

The word deceitful can also represent the way in which the wrong desire to be rich deceives people. These deceptions will steal their time and attention which instead should be placed on the condition of their own soil (mind), the reason for their inability to manifest the fruit hidden in the seed (message).

> **22** The thorny soil that received the seed is like one that considers what is being said, the teachings, mandates, precepts, and decrees of God, however, they are full of anxiety letting the cares of the world distract their attention from the seed to their present situation, they let the problem override the promise, deception steps in because of the delusion of money from the worlds perspective, then, as a result of their soil (mind) being full of thorns, the thorns press in all around the seed and suffocate (strangle) the seeds future and they remain barren, unfruitful, never yielding what they ought to. (DHP)

They have never learned, let alone applied the truths in **1 Peter 5:7**:

7 Casting all your care upon him; for he careth for you.

7 Casting all your cares [all your anxieties, all your worries, and all your concerns, once and for all] on Him, for He cares about you [with deepest affection, and watches over you very carefully]. (Amplified Bible)

> **7** Throw the entirety, every anxious distraction, anything that would disunite (affect your unity) with him and his word, take your rest in him, He takes great interest in you and he cares about the things you have need of. (DHP)

King David (the psalmist) echoes the same sentiment as the Apostle Peter penned:

Psalm 55:22

22 Cast thy burden upon the LORD, and he shall sustain thee: he shall never suffer the righteous to be moved.

Cast every care, burden, trial, persecution, and affliction upon the Lord. Why? He will hold you up, He will sustain you as go through it. However, this promise is to the righteous. Yes, His death, burial, and resurrection over sin, sickness and the grave gave us His righteousness (see **2 Corinthians 5:21**), however, we still must walk in and operate through our right standing with Him.

The word **righteous** in **Verse 22** is the Hebrew word, "*tsaddîyq*" (pronounced: tsad-deek') and translates as, "right/righteous in government, cause, conduct, character, correct, and lawful. As you well know, there are those who Christ has made His righteousness available to, but at present are not demonstrating/walking in it. The promise of not "being moved" belongs to them. The Hebrew word for **moved** is "*môṭ*" (pronounced: mote') and describes someone who cannot be, "shaken, overthrown, or dislodged."

The Apostle Paul in writing to the church in Philippi exhorted with the same thoughts when he wrote his letter to them:

Philippians 4:6-7

6 Be careful for nothing; but in everything by prayer and supplication with thanksgiving let your requests be made known unto God.

The word **careful** is the Greek word, "*merimnaō*" (pronounced: mer-im-nah'-o) which speaks of not becoming anxious (side note: many today are on strong anxiety drugs that only numb them and mask the true issue and can lead to serious mental and physical issues), becoming completely occupied with the wrong thoughts.

Adam Clarke said in his commentary, anxiety cannot change the state or condition of anything from bad to good, but will infallibly injure your own souls. If we will learn and implement this truth, look at the promises in **Verse 7**.

7 And the peace of God, which passeth all understanding, shall keep your hearts and minds through Christ Jesus.

Releasing the cares of this life will keep us in peace, it will keep your heart and mind as we learn to operate in the Mind of Christ (see **1 Corinthians 2:16**) which we now have access to.

The word **keep** is powerful in the Greek language, it is the word, "*phroureō*" (pronounced: froo-reh'-o) and defines as, "to guard, to protect by a military guard, to prevent a hostile invasion, to place a guard as a sentinel (a soldier/guard whose job is to stand and keep watch).

The Thorny ground (soil) will quickly respond at first, then they are overcome with worries, greed, worldly desires (as they have not yet died to their flesh), offense, wrong choices, and decisions which all will choke the seed (word), effecting their spiritual life to the point no spiritual fruit is developed.

Notice our text passage again that began this chapter, **Verse 7**, the seed was sown, the message was preached, but that soil was full of thorns which overtook the seed.

Being consumed with cares and worries steals all their time and demands their attention so they have no time to honestly look at the condition of their own soil. This type of soil is never satisfied because it always demands more, enough is never enough. The temptation becomes overwhelming to being dishonest, to cheat, to do whatever it takes to get more, even using and taking advantage of others. Money in/of itself is not evil, how one gets it, that is another story. The Bible reminds us:

1 Timothy 6:10

"The love of money is the root of all evil: which while some coveted after, they have erred from the faith, and pierced themselves through with many sorrows."

The riches/cares of this world entice with an ungodly allurement which will always promise something it cannot and will not deliver. Some speak of the happiness/joy that money brings, but when gained, especially the world's way, it brings sorrow. Herein lies the difference, God's way versus the world's way.

Albert Barnes penned these powerful thoughts in his commentary, *"How many, O how many, thus foolishly drown themselves in destruction and perdition! How many more might reach heaven, if it were not for this deep-seated love of that which fills the mind with care, deceives the soul, and finally leaves it naked, and guilty, and lost!"*

There is a right way, a kingdom way to receive God's abundance, yet it must be done His way through His word. This may take more time in the natural, you have seed…time…then…harvest. You have to receive the seed, let it become planted, water the seed, sun the seed, weed around the seed, and as the root system becomes established deep in the soil, the fruit springs up, matures, then harvested.

Proverbs 10:22

22 The blessing of the LORD, it maketh rich, and he addeth no sorrow with it.

> 22 When the Lord is the source of blessing, when his prosperity becomes your prosperity, it comes with this promise, his way brings his results with no worldly sorrow (painful toiling, hardship, or grievous labor). (DHP)

The thorny soil describes the unproductive/fruitless lives of individuals who allow the cares of life to take precedence in their mind, consuming their thoughts instead of taking those thoughts captive. Then, the thorns suffocate the seeds' potential that they heard, and no fruit ever develops. Discouragement sets in, the blame game starts, pointing fingers at everyone and everything, never thinking they might need to look inward, into their own soil (mind) as to the hindrance.

Do we still not discern or understand starting in Genesis (the book of beginnings) and on, soil played a very key, important role throughout the scriptures? We came from dirt, our first parents, Adam and Eve were gardeners, responsible to cultivate (farm, develop, and plow) the very ground they/we came from. Then, the amazing thing is Jesus's stories of agriculture, farming, seed, soil, and harvest describing/explaining the kingdom.

———

As we close out this chapter, I pray for you, the reader and myself.

"Lord let the scales be removed from our eyes. We give Holy Spirit permission to take us deep into the hidden recesses of our soil, mind, and heart. Convict us of operating in any soil but that which You call good. Show us, then we will act, respond, acknowledge, and change our heart condition. We know that You do not condemn, You convict for our good. Today will begin a new day, a new soil will emerge, and a different outcome is eminent.
The fruit that comes will be mature, fully developed because of the right soil, and it will remain. It will not rot, or come to ruin. It will be a blessing in our lives as well as all that we encounter on this journey. In the name of Jesus, we call it done, and give You all the praise and glory for finishing the work in/through us that You began.
The fruit that is coming will bring glory to Your name. The past is forgiven, forgotten, removed and is no longer a hindrance to my purpose, calling and destiny. Amen and amen!

CHAPTER ELEVEN
THE GOOD GROUND

Matthew 13:8,23

8 But other fell into good ground, and brought forth fruit, some an hundredfold, some sixtyfold, some thirtyfold.

8 And finally, some seed came to rest in good ground (excellent in its nature and characteristics, therefore well adapted to produce the fruit, the end result of the seeds' purpose), the soil was rich and fertile causing fruit to come forth because the seed produced it fullest potential (which is 100), others 60, and some 30. (DHP)

AN INTERESTING THOUGHT HERE: IN THIS KINGDOM PARABLE, Jesus stated the good (best) soil receiving this message (seed) had the potential of 100-fold, then He stated others in the "same soil" only experienced 60-fold, and some only 30-fold. God is not a respecter of persons, but He is of principles. He does not value one more important than another. So, the person receiving

100-fold, 60-fold, or 30-fold in good ground would lend itself to believe that the individual determines what measure of the message they are going to receive.

Do they hear, then settle for a 60-fold or 30-fold return (harvest)? Do our thoughts, words, and actions on the message sown into our soil set boundaries hindering the seed's full potential? Do we settle for 60 because we have never experienced what it is like to enjoy the 100, or 30 in view of never experiencing the 60? Our words can stunt the seeds' potential, or release the seeds' fullest potential.

In Biblical numerics, the number 100 speaks of being children of promise. Why settle for anything less than the best He has promised? Also notice in this kingdom parable, Jesus starts with 100, then goes down from there. Often, I hear ministers reference this as 30, 60, and 100-fold, however, in this parable, Jesus reveals the seed's capacity beginning with the best, 100-fold.

23 But he that received seed into the good ground is he that heareth the word, and understandeth *it;* which also beareth fruit, and bringeth forth, some an hundredfold, some sixty, some thirty.

> **23** Those who receive the message into good ground, those whose heart, mind, and soil are prepared and are willing to allow the seed to fully develop and grow to maturity. They take the necessary time to hear, consider, understand, and perceive the language of the kingdom, the promised end result is a life full of continual fruit bearing, beginning with the best, 100-fold. (DHP)

————

WHILE LOOKING AT THESE TWO VERSES SOMETHING GRABBED MY attention that I had missed in the research, study, and writing of this new manuscript. So I went back and reread the usage of the certain words, uncovering something I had missed.

Matthew 13:4,5,7,8

Verse 4 "some seeds fell **by (Greek-beside, near)** the wayside…"

Verse 5 "Some fell **upon (Greek-against, towards)** stony places…"

Verse 7 "And some fell **among (Greek-same words as upon)** thorns…"

Verse 8 "But other fell **into (Greek-in the presence of, immediately upon, came to rest in/on)** good ground…"

The seed was the same in this kingdom parable, the word of God (seed) is called incorruptible (it cannot decay, come to ruin, it is imperishable). The Sower scattered (sowed) the seed but it fell among four different soils (if you will, four different types of people). The first seed fell "**by**" the wayside, the second fell "**upon**" the stony places, the third fell "**among**" the thorns, and the fourth fell "**into**" good ground.

Notice the meaning of the four soils from the Greek listed above. Seed **beside or near** will not work, seed **against or towards** will not produce, seed **among (against, towards)** will not completely develop, but the seed that comes **into the presence of**, that **comes into and rests in/on** the good soil comes to maturity.

The good soil represents disciples in the truest sense of the word; they are students, pupils, listeners, and learners. They understand the process, and at times, the suffering they will go through for a season. They understand that purging/pruning seasons are not punishment, but preparation.

When was the last time we honestly assessed our own discipleship? How do we hear, yet even more important, receive and act on God's Word? Our reception of this kingdom message and the fruit that should follow is determined by the condition of our soil (heart, soul). It is not based on the messenger (five-fold, ascension giftings).

Have we prepared our hearts to receive it, then allow the process of the seed to work in/under the soil (the unseen realm), giving it the time needed to bring externally the DNA that resides in the seed internally?

Let us look at two of the gospels that both reference the **good** versus evil **heart**.

Matthew 12:33-35

33 Either make the **tree good**, and his **fruit good**; or else make the **tree corrupt**, and **his fruit** corrupt: for **the tree is known by** *his* **fruit**.

> **33** There are two expressions of a tree, if it is good (moral, virtuous, honest), its fruit (offspring) will be the same, if it is corrupt (rotten, impure) on the inside, its fruit will be tainted, damaged, putrefied (decayed, rotten, producing an extremely unpleasant smell), each tree is known by what its intimacy produces. (DHP)

Another thought of interest to reflect on concerning the wording of **Verse 33** in the KJV. Jesus refers to the good tree as, "**his**," the corrupt tree as, "**his**," and the fruit of both as, "**his**" three times in this verse, calling the tree a gender. I believe the prophetic implication here is referencing the tree as people and what type of fruit they produce.

This might be a stretch for some, but look at this passage in light of the above comment:

Mark 8:22-25

22 And he cometh to Bethsaida; and they bring a blind man unto him, and besought him to touch him.

23 And he took the blind man by the hand, and led him out of the town; and when he had spit on his eyes, and put his hands upon him, he asked him if he saw ought.

24 And he looked up, and said, **I see men as trees, walking**.

25 After that he put *his* hands again upon his eyes, and made him look up: and he was restored, and saw every man clearly.

Interestingly enough, during his healing process he sees men as trees.

The works will resemble the heart: nothing good can proceed from an evil spirit; no good fruit can proceed from a corrupt heart. Before the heart of man can produce any good, it must be renewed and influenced by the Spirit of God. (Adam Clarke Commentary)

The tree is not known because of its leaves, its form, width, height, or its bark (the outer covering), it is known by the fruit it produces. The DNA (blueprint) of a tree is designed to grow, develop, mature, and manifest the fruit **externally** of what already exists **internally**.

Matthew 12:34-35

34 O generation of vipers, how can ye, being evil, speak good things? for out of the abundance of the heart the mouth speaketh.

> **34** You are the offspring of wicked men, which is why your words are like a poisonous serpent as was theirs, the mouth will always reveal what is in the heart, in the right situation, when the heat gets turned up, if unresolved issues and conflicts are still hidden within, the mouth will give voice to the intents and purposes the heart carries. (DHP)

35 A good man out of the good treasure of the heart bringeth forth good things: and an evil man out of the evil treasure bringeth forth evil things.

> **35** The good, upright, virtuous, and honorable man will reveal all the valuable, precious treasure that he has deposited within, then will be seen by all, and the same is true of the evil (unethical) man, the fleshly, carnal man, destitute of morals and the Spirit, what comes out of him will expose his true nature. (DHP)

Luke 6:43-45

43 For a good tree bringeth not forth corrupt fruit; neither doth a corrupt tree bring forth good fruit.

43 A tree that is genuine, useful, honorable, and noble does not bring forth rotten fruit, unfit for use, nor does a corrupt (impure) tree bear/produce valuable precious fruit. (DHP)

44 For every tree is known by his own fruit. For of thorns men do not gather figs, nor of a bramble bush gather they grapes.

44 Every tree produces from what it is intimate with, what it is intimate with privately will be seen publicly. Thorns and briars cannot harvest figs, neither can shrubs full of thorns harvest grapes. (DHP)

Good and Bad Fruit.—Christ here speaks of the inner nature—the heart—of man and of its outward manifestations, and asserts that in all cases the inner is the maker of the outward. A good heart will infallibly reveal itself in holiness of word and deed: in like manner an evil heart will disclose itself, in spite of all hypocritical attempts to conceal the true state of matters. (Preachers Homiletical Commentary)

The Greek word for **tree** in **Verse 44** is, "*hekastos*" (pronounced: hek'-as-tos) which also defines as, "every man and woman."

45 A good man out of the good treasure of his heart bringeth forth that which is good; and an evil man out of the evil treasure of his heart bringeth forth that which is evil: for of the abundance of the heart his mouth speaketh.

45 The good man who is upright and virtuous brings forth and produces what is profitable, that good which he has stored up in his mind will be made manifest and seen for the excellent qualities it possesses. The evil man whose nature, character, and motives are unethical can/will only reveal the DNA of those wicked, unsound, flaws in his storehouse because his mind has never been renewed. The good man and evil man will both make known what is hidden in their heart as that which fills the heart (mind), their lips will give voice to what the mind is filled with. (DHP)

The word **heart** is the Greek word, "*kardia*" (pronounced: kar-dee'-ah) which also refers to the, "thoughts or feelings of the mind, of the soul so far as it is affected and stirred in a bad way or good, or of the soul as the seat of the sensibilities, affections, emotions, desires, appetites, passions."

The word **mouth** in Thayer's G4750 is the Greek word, "*stoma*" (pronounced: stom'-a), it states, "since thoughts of a man's soul find verbal utterance by his mouth, the "heart" or "soul" and the mouth are distinguished."

At this point in writing this chapter, I was once again reminded of a portion of scripture that will further our understanding of fruit.

James 5:7-8

7 Be patient therefore, brethren, unto the coming of the Lord. Behold, the husbandman waiteth for the precious fruit of the earth, and hath long patience for it, until he receive the early and latter rain.

> 7 Do not lose heart my brothers, but patiently and bravely endure misfortune, and trouble, stay in the spirit, the presence and appearance of the Lord is at hand, the farmer (husbandman) is looking for and expecting the valuable and costly (of a great

> price) fruit from the field (ground) in which it was planted. The farmer does not lose heart during the seeds process from its planting to its fruit (harvest), he knows that the end result, the mature fruit, must first go through two seasons of rain, the **early** (first) rain and the **latter** (2nd) rain, the seed of your deliverance has already been sown. (DHP)

IN THE NATURAL, ISRAEL IS KNOWN TO HAVE TWO MAIN rainfalls a year. The early rain (former) which happens in October, and the latter rain which falls in March and April just before the harvest. (Also see **Joel 2:23.**)

8 Be ye also patient; stablish your hearts: for the coming of the Lord draweth nigh.

> **8** You too must remain patient just as the farmer does, take courage, do not be cast down during the seed's process and the trials you will experience, the appearing of the Lord and what he planted **IN YOU** is at hand. (DHP)

Let me add to the foundation being laid in this chapter, let's re-look at **John 15:1-8** (italics added for emphasis):

1 I am the true vine, and **my Father is the husbandman.**

2 Every branch in me that beareth not fruit he taketh away: and **every _branch_ that beareth fruit, he purgeth it, that it may bring forth more fruit.**

3 Now **ye are clean through the word** which I have spoken unto you.

4 Abide in me, and I in you. As **the branch cannot bear fruit of itself, except it abide in the vine**; no more can ye, except ye abide in me.

5 I am the vine, ye *are* **the branches**: He that abideth in me, and I in him, the same bringeth forth much fruit: for without me ye can do nothing.

6 If a man abide not in me, he is cast forth as a branch, and is withered; and men gather them, and cast *them* into the fire, and they are burned.

7 If ye abide in me, and my words abide in you, ye shall ask what ye will, and it shall be done unto you.

8 Herein is my Father glorified, that ye bear much fruit; so shall ye be my disciples.

In the Apostle John's letter in the gospels, he speaks to the Godhead's function and responsibilities as well as the branches. God as the farmer planted, He planted in Eden, He planted His son as a seed into the earth, which is the vine (**Galatians 3:16**), then redemption put that seed (Christ) in us. Now, we have become the branches which the vine produces.

Verse 2 expresses the purpose/process of purging, it is not a disciplinarian action but a preparation (preparing) us for the next season of manifesting more fruit. **More** is the Greek word, "*pleion*" (pronounced: pli-own) which defines as, "more in quality, quantity, more excellent, superior."

To produce fruit, the branches (us) must **abide** (Greek word, "*meno*" which means to, "remain, to stay in the presence of, to dwell") IN HIM (the vine). This does not happen in one hour of corporate worship and word on Sunday! It is a lifestyle, it is a student, disciple, a studier (not just a reader) of God's Word. The promise for the abiding branch is "much fruit" (**Verse 5**).

Verse 8 shares the Father's heart, he is glorified when his children produce, bear, and reveal fruit. He ends the verse with the phrase, "so shall you be my disciples." The reference here is what true discipleship looks like, they have stayed planted in the good soil, they have passed the tests and trials that came their way, their character remained intact (not damaged or impaired), fruit is the trophy of faithful discipleship.

Consider this:

The Father God is the farmer (Husbandman).

Jesus is the True Vine.

The Holy Spirit is the life source (the sap that circulates in the vascular system of the plant) which flows from the vine (Jesus). He is the oil.

The Ekklesia (the true church, the many-membered body of Christ) is the branches of the vine where ultimately the fruit comes through.

The good soil has not been beaten or trodden by the feet of men, there are no stones or thorns in it. It has been well plowed, tilled, and fertilized which describes honest- hearted hearers who are led by the Spirit, those who have spiritual understanding because of their prayer and study time.

They have not just heard these truths, they have lived them out through life's struggles and attacks, they understand the process and are all the better for it. Their life, choices, and actions have allowed the seed to remain from the planting (sowing) process till it is matured and ready for harvest. Their soil (mind, heart) is rich, clutter free, and revealing the 100-fold return as promised by the Lord in this parable.

They have totally submitted themselves to the Truth, refusing to allow the cares and anxieties of this life to overtake the seeds' potential. The seeds' root system runs deep as there is nothing in their soil to hinder its full production. And finally, the seed's harvest leaves no room to doubt their soil condition.

FINAL THOUGHTS

As I close out my final thoughts on *The Kingdom, The Seed, & The Soil,* I am overcome with all kinds of emotion, joy, tears, and a true sense of the word humble and what it really means. Never on my best days could I have ever produced the insight, the revelation, or the scriptures in the order that Holy Spirit released them to me.

All the times awakened at 4AM and 5AM, compelled to get up, go into my living room or office with my legal pad and write down the scriptures, the stories in the Word, the thoughts that Holy Spirit had impressed on my mind in those early hours, then penned in this book. I have learned, relearned, and unlearned so much through this Kingdom endeavor. The cry of my heart is that as you have read, studied, and prayed as you journeyed through this book, that you have allowed Holy Spirit to challenge you as to what you must "let go of," and what you must, "grab a hold of," what areas need to be realigned and refocused.

My greatest desire is that you, the reader, allowed Holy Spirit to reveal your present soil, not from the point of condemnation, but for its removal and change, if necessary. That your greatest days, manifestations, growth, and fruit are in front of you, you will/are going from "faith to faith" and "glory to glory."

If this book has helped or blessed you in any way, please feel free to email me at: ddh1020@cox.net. We overcome the enemy by the "Blood of the Lamb and the word of (in) or testimony **(Revelation 12:11)**.

————

IT HAPPENED AGAIN:

January 3, 2024 @ 4:40AM, the Holy Spirit woke me up and said, *"You are not finished, there is one more thing I want to show you, and then add it to the book."*

I thought I was finished with this manuscript. I have gone through a soft edit twice, preparing to send it to my publisher/editor. Upon awakening out of my sleep, Holy Spirit once again revealed the finishing stroke of His brush to be put on the canvas of His work through His servant. He said, *"Religion and its tradition is the seed killer!"* That immediately grabbed my attention and I responded, *"Show me."* He then took me to the following scriptures and once again, THE Teacher taught a teacher.

Mark 7:1-9,13-16

In **Verses 1-9**, Jesus begins to challenge the traditions of the Pharisees (the religious hierarchy of His day) because they began to complain that Jesus's disciples did not keep **their** traditions by washing their hands before they ate. His response in addressing their accusation was epic. In essence, He said, "Yep. Isaiah prophesied that this day would come, and here it is." (**Isaiah 29:13.**)

Here are the bullet points of His discourse with them:

- Your lips say one thing, your heart says another (**John 2:23-25, Jeremiah 17:9-10**).
- Your worship of me is in vain, as you teach your traditions (doctrines of men), rejecting the commandments of God.
- You allow your traditions to override and reject My commandments so you can keep your tradition.

Then, in **Verse 13**, He expounds on the outcome of operating in religious traditions at the expense of rejecting the Word of God (Seed).

Your tradition - D, later Syriac in the margin, Saxon, and all the Itala but one, add τη μωρα, by your Foolish tradition, your foolish law: - Anglo-Saxon. (Adam Clarke Commentary)[1]

13 Making the word of God of none effect through your tradition, which ye have delivered: and many such like things do ye.

> **13 Your** (highlighted for emphasis) religious traditions disannul (they cancel), they invalidate, and deprive the Word of God of its force and authority, rendering it void of results, these traditions that you entrust to your

disciples through your teachings actually puts them in the same prison as you. (DHP)

WHAT DEFILES A PERSON

14 And when he had called all the people unto him, he said unto them, Hearken unto me every one of you, and understand:

> **14** Then, he turned to the other group (some translations speak of the common people, not the Pharisees that stood further away) and spoke to them saying, "give ear to what I am saying, thoroughly comprehend it and you will be able to judge correctly and become spiritually wise." (DHP)

Jesus then explains to them what the Pharisees could not and would not hear, being steeped in their own traditions, and as the saying goes, "not being able to see the forest because of the trees." (A Renaissance proverb collection written by John Heywood, 1546)[2]

15 There is nothing from without a man, that entering into him can defile him: but the things which come out of him, those are they that defile the man.

> **15** It is not the external things, food, drink, washing of the hands or not, those things which go into the body or the external cleansing that defile or make one unclean or unholy. It is not what goes in the mouth but what comes out of the mouth which begin in the heart, the actions are

a result of the heart (soil) issues, which is what pollutes and desecrates the man. (DHP)

———

He continues to exhort them by saying that they need a "hearing" ear concerning these principles and truths.

16 If any man have ears to hear, let him hear.

> **16** Every man with the mental and physical capacity to [hear], he should give audience to these things until he understands (comprehends) them. (DHP)

Jesus used the word "tradition" in **Verse 13** and it has unbelievable prophetic insight and application. Every letter of the Greek alphabet has a numeric value. When you add up the sum total of each letter and its numeric value of the word, *"tradition,"* it totals 6...6...6 (666) which is the number that speaks of the spirit of antichrist. There are two Greek words that make up the word antichrist. "An-tee" & "Khris-tos." The spirit of antichrist is anyone or anything that opposes the anointing and presence of Christ. It is a spirit! Religious traditions are anti-Christ!

———

TWO MORE THOUGHTS AS HOLY SPIRIT GAVE THEM TO ME THIS MORNING:

2 Timothy 3:1-6

The Apostle Paul warned and challenged his son in the Lord, Timothy, to watch for these signs as stated ' in **verses 1-5**. Growing up in church, I always heard these things were manifestations of the world, not the church at the end of an age. Yet **verse 6** reveals who the subject matter was referring to, that will operate in these things apart from God.

6 Having a form of godliness, but denying the power thereof: from such turn away.

The Greek word **form** is "*morphōsis*" (pronounced: mor'-fo-sis) which describes, "an appearance, semblance (the outward appearance or apparent form of something, especially when the reality is different), the external form."

Religion and its traditions are an "empty" look alike. It is a form which allows them to live as an external shell that resembles, yet has no internal substance, strength, power and ability (*dunamis*) —that is the game changer and the fruit producer. Paul's final exhortation was, *"From such turn away."*

Avoid them, shun them, do not associate with them, they are seed (destiny, purpose, and fruit) killers.

———

ONE MORE THOUGHT ON SEED KILLERS:

Jesus was rejected in His own hometown and by His own countrymen.

Mark 6:1-6

Jesus is teaching in His hometown on the sabbath and His disciples are with Him. At first, the people are astonished at His words, His wisdom, and the mighty works done through His hands. Then the rumblings began, *"Isn't he just a carpenter, isn't Mary his mother, aren't those his brothers, James, Joses, Juda, and Simon, and his sisters are here too?"* Then here it comes: "They were offended (repulsed, to judge unjustly) at Him."

"Who does He think He is?"

Jesus then declares familiarity is the seed killer of the prophet and the prophetic. What was the result (outcome)? There (in that setting, in that soil), the Word made Flesh (Jesus) could not function to His/its full potential. One translation says that, "He could only heal a few folks with minor aliments...". WOW!!!

How quick did the offense come once the seed had been spoken? Immediately! Throughout this manuscript, more than once we have penned that Jesus told His disciples that satan comes immediately to steal the seed before it can take root. The seed was rejected, then removed, and the result, NO MIGHTY WORKS, NO FRUIT!

6 And he marvelled because of their unbelief. And he went round about the villages, teaching.

> **6** He was astonished (stunned, dismayed, appalled) at their disbelief, faithlessness, and their lack of trust and confidence, so he continued going from town-to-town imparting, instilling his kingdom message, never allowing opposition to hinder his mission. (DHP)

THE DIFFERENCE BETWEEN DOUBT AND UNBELIEF.

Doubt simply defines as ignorance because of a lack of information. You just do not know. However, unbelief is dangerous. It is a decision to reject what you have heard or seen. You cannot operate in unbelief until **after** you have heard, then comes the decision to reject it (unbelief) or receive it (faith).

Unbelief will stop, thwart (prevent from accomplishing) the seed you just heard sown; therefore, the seed's DNA never manifests in the soil that rejected it. Selah!

And of course, it happened one more time in Riveria, Texas, just after lunch time as I was preparing to speak the fourth service for my friend, Apostle Ronny Robinson, *Firm Foundations Church* on January 9, 2024.

I was releasing this message as the first fruits of this manuscript in his church, and later that week for my spiritual son at his church in Falfurrias, Texas, Pastor August Patroelj. Once again, preparing for that evening service, I felt compelled by the Holy Spirt to relook at the **Genesis 3:15** prophecy and the few verses that followed. And then one more time, January 20th, 5AM, Holy Spirit added the final thoughts for this book.

Genesis 3:14-19

14 And the LORD God said unto the serpent, Because thou hast done this, thou *art* cursed above all cattle, and above every beast of the field; upon thy belly shalt thou go, and dust shalt thou eat all the days of thy life:

15 And I will put enmity between thee and the woman, and between thy seed and her seed; it shall bruise thy head, and thou shalt bruise his heel.

16 Unto the woman he said, I will greatly multiply thy sorrow and thy conception; in sorrow thou shalt bring forth children; and thy desire *shall be* to thy husband, and he shall rule over thee.

17 And unto Adam he said, Because thou hast hearkened unto the voice of thy wife, and hast eaten of the tree, of which I commanded thee, saying, Thou shalt not eat of it: cursed *is* the ground for thy sake; in sorrow shalt thou eat *of* it all the days of thy life;

18 Thorns also and thistles shall it bring forth to thee; and thou shalt eat the herb of the field;

19 In the sweat of thy face shalt thou eat bread, till thou return unto the ground; for out of it wast thou taken: for dust thou *art,* and unto dust shalt thou return.

The prophecy had three parts: first to Lucifer, second to Eve, and the third to Adam. We have already looked at the first part, spoken to Lucifer concerning the "seed" that was coming in depth in this book.

After God spoke to Lucifer, He then turned and said to Eve, *"I will greatly multiply thy sorrow and thy conception; in sorrow thou shalt bring forth children; and thy desire shall be to thy husband, and he shall rule over thee."* These words spoken over her would be the result of her disobedience in eating from the one tree they were told not to partake of, the tree of the knowledge of good and evil (**Genesis 2:9**).

Here is what was revealed early the morning of the 20ᵗʰ. I believe there are a few points of great importance and insight that must be examined:

1) Her action upon deception, because of the words spoken by the serpent, ultimately revealed the result that befell the world, and all that would be born from that point on because of their now fallen nature.

2) Hardship, sorrow, worry, and pain had now been loosed into the earth (from the Hebrew), all of these will be the consequences once you conceive, carry, then birth.

3) This fallen nature that Eve and Adam now manifested would be on/in every child born into the present world because of the world's now sin-riddled, fear-based, death doomed makeup. Every child will manifest the same sorrow that the parents now carried and released. Their intimacy would not produce joy, but sorrow, hardship, and pain.

4) And finally, Eve's longing would be only for her husband, Adam, and he will rule, exercise dominion over her and she will live solely at the will and pleasure of her husband. The equality of the two had now changed. This was NOT God's original intent or purpose for earth's first parents.

————

Now after speaking to Eve, God puts his focus on Adam saying: "Because thou hast hearkened unto the voice of thy wife, and hast eaten of the tree, of which I commanded thee, saying, Thou shalt not eat of it: cursed *is* the ground for thy sake; in sorrow shalt thou eat *of* it all the days of thy life; Thorns also and thistles shall it bring forth to thee; and thou shalt eat the herb of the field; In the sweat of thy face shalt thou eat bread, till thou return unto the ground; for out of it wast thou taken: for dust thou *art,* and unto dust shalt thou return." **(Verses 17-19)**

These few verses also reveal some interesting thoughts and patterns pertaining to their present situation, BUT GOD HAD A PLAN:

1) The ground (soil) that was once pure, clean, and free from any issues was now painfully and sorrowfully cursed.

2) The fallen Adamic nature was now manifest and operating in the earth, and now, since that nature was being revealed, Adam would only be able to partake from the cursed soil, and all cursed soil could produce to consume.

3) Then God stated that the once perfect soil (ground) now as a result of the present curse would only harvest thorns and thistles and he would only eat the "herb of the field (John Gill Commentary says, "he would eat the same thing the beasts of the field ate."

4) And finally, his life would result in toil, turmoil, and hard labor until he returned to the ground from which he was made. His face would be toward the cursed soil as a continual reminder of his present condition. Every time he looked at it, it would continually remind him and reinforce his fall, failure, and prophecy.

God knew Adam would fall, but remember, He had a plan before the foundation of the earth. In His mind, the Lamb had already been slain to restore fallen man back to God's original intent for him (**Revelation 13:8**). He formed His man to rule and reign, and to manifest the Kingdom of Heaven into/upon the earth), which would be a redeemed man, given the mind of Christ (**1 Corinthians 2:16**). So the soil had to be involved in redemption, as we have shown in this book that the mind (heart) is also a reference to the soil. Thus, Jesus teaching the Kingdom Parable of the Sower revealed that once again, a new redeemed, fertile soil is available for His new-creation man.

The Apostle Paul wrote to the church in Rome and declared that all of creation is in travail and groanings (birthing terms), waiting for the appearing, the revealing, and the revelation of the sons (Greek-"*uihos*" pronounced: kwee-os, which speaks of fully grown seasoned sons) walking in maturity, revealing and living the revelation of sonship once again before the world like Adam in his original state. In Christ, we have now been delivered from the corruption that the cursed soil produced, hindering the maturing of full-grown sons. The earth (soil) had been travailing, and groaning in birth pains until the redemption was complete. Adam's fallen nature had been restored to Christ's "many sons" and once again, we are now clothed with the glory, just as God's created son Adam was before his fall.

His servant by choice,
Dr. Don Hughes
REV House School of Ministry (RHSOM.com)
Rev House Fellowship (Broken Arrow, OK, House Church)

1. Clarke, A. (1869). Clarke's Commentary: The Holy Bible, containing the Old and New Testaments: The Text printed from the most correct copies of the Present Authorized Translation, including the marginal readings and parallel texts, with a Commentary and Critical Notes.
2. Daniela Mcleod, "Cannot see the forest for the trees," Grammarist, accessed January 20, 2024, https://grammarist.com/usage/cannot-see-the-forest-for-the-trees

SECTION TWO

AN EXHORTATION TO ALL MINISTRY GIFTS

To all Apostles, Prophets, Evangelists, Pastors, and Teachers, Home Bible study fellowships, Church leadership training, Schools of Ministry, and Sunday School teachers. The following is a detailed outline that I wrote from this manuscript.

You have my permission to scan these pages, or request a pdf (ddh1020@cox.net) if you have purchased the Book and Study Guide to develop and teach as the Lord would lead you. My only request is that you would consider sowing a seed into this Kingdom endeavor as I believe this message should be taken to the Ekklesia (Church) around the world. I also believe that the truths revealed in this manuscript can be life changing. When you see **DHP**, remember that is my paraphrase of the verse or verses, those can be found in this book in each chapter that parallels with this outline (you can add them to your notes if you so desire).

Listed on the bottom of this page are the different ways you can sow.

Kingdom blessings to all that you set your hand to:

Dr. Don Hughes
Founder Rev House School of Ministry
(RHSOM.com)
Team Lead at Rev House Fellowship
Broken Arrow, OK

Paypal.me/drdondhughes
Venmo: @Don-Hughes-22
CashApp: @DonHughes
Also, Credit/Debit Card

Or mail a check to:
23005 E. 103rd PL. S.
Broken Arrow, OK 74014

I) WHY DID JESUS SPEAK IN PARABLES?

LESSON 1

First, let us define what a parable is from the Greek language. It is the Greek word, *"parabole"* (pronounced: par-ab-ol-ay), it translates as, "the comparison of one thing with another, a likeness, a similitude, an example by which either the duties of men or the things of God, particularly, the nature and history of God's kingdom are figuratively portrayed." Simply put, "a parable is an **earthly story** with a **heavenly meaning**."

Some History

In **Matthew 3:16-17**, Jesus is baptized by John the Baptist in the Jordan river, the heavens open and God acknowledges and declares Him as His son. Jesus goes into the wilderness temptation and comes out victorious over every test that the enemy presented Him with. In **Matthew 4:17**, He establishes His purpose and message, to challenge the mindsets of the religious systems/structures of His day by preaching the message of the kingdom.

Matthew 3:16-17, 4:17,23 (KJV & DHP)

God reveals the seed mentioned in the first prophecy spoken in the Bible from God himself in **Genesis 3:14-15**.

In **Matthew 4:17**, Jesus speaks of his purpose and destiny. In **Verse 23**, he continues teaching his message in the synagogue.

Acts 1:3 (KJV & **DHP**)

After His resurrection, He spent another 40 days being seen by many before His ascension and His last words echoed the message He began with. He never veered off course from His mission or His message.

The right message brings the right manifestations.

Matthew 24:14 (KJV & **DHP**)

A Provoking Thought from Dr. Munroe

I was watching a video message from Dr. Myles Munroe sometime back, and he made a statement that caught my attention to the point that I stopped the video and thought about his comment. He said, *"God doesn't automatically volunteer information (revelation)."* As I considered his words, immediately some scriptures came to mind. In Matthew's gospel, Jesus spoke about asking, seeking, and knocking and then revealed those who "ask receive, those who seek find, and those who knock, the door will open (**Matthew 7:7-8**)."

Matthew 7:7-8 (KJV & **DHP**)

There are many other scriptures, stories, and references to the individual having a part to play in receiving their answer, their need met, even their miracle. Jesus asks the man with the thirty-eight-year infirmity at the pool of Bethesda what he wanted, "Do you want to be made whole?" Jesus gave very direct commands to him after he made his excuses, "rise, pick up your bed and walk" The man had to respond, he had to act on Jesus words, when he did his part, Jesus did his part (**John 5:1-9**).

SEE THE FOLLOWING STORIES AND SCRIPTURES FOR MORE CONFIRMATION:

2 Kings 5:1-14, Mark 10:46-52, Luke 18:1-8, Proverbs 8:17, Hebrews 11:6, James 5:7.

II) YOUR PURSUIT & SOIL DETERMINE (DICTATES) THE FRUIT

LESSON 2

There is a concept in the New Testament that must be examined as we move forward. Jesus never had a problem gathering a multitude or getting a crowd, for a myriad of reasons, either based on His reputation, the miracles he manifested, and at times the "free lunch" program (this will be brought to light further in this chapter). It brings up an honest question. Why were they following Him? Why are we following Him?

Perform a few miracles, get your name out there, raise the dead, cast out some devils, and His reputation would produce crowds, multitudes (See **John 6:2**), which one day produced a crowd of 5000 men (plus women and children, they did not count them back then). There was only one little boy's lunch, Jesus took it, blessed it, and again, performed another miracle. The "free lunch program" started (kind of like today's coffee and donut churches), and Jesus' statement in **John 6:26** exposed the heart/soil of them. (Read **Verses 22-26, KJV & DHP Verse 26**)

The Multitudes, the 70, the 12, the 3, and the 1

Miracles, reputation, and food produced the multitudes and initially seventy other disciples, plus the twelve, they all were pursuing, as to what/why, well that is being explained in these first two chapters. If you continue reading all of **John 6**, some insightful things are seen. After expressing His thoughts as to why they were following Him (**Verse 26** above), the challenge/separation comes to those who were following and why. In **Verses 53-58**, He begins the discourse, the challenge to their pursuit.

I believe He was revealing "**Covenant 101**" to them, the free lunch program was over, their pursuit and what they were pursuing was going to be taken to the next level, or at least uncovered. He was not speaking of cannibalism, he was referencing covenant, from then on, they had to pursue **Him** (not what he gave them), he was offering them the God life, his nature, power, and all God given power and ability.

Their response in **Verse 60** showed where they were. "This is a hard saying; who can hear it?" (see **DHP Verse 60**)

Jesus never played favorites, He lived by principles and responded often to man's pursuit, those (His disciples) who pursued Him the most got the closest to Him. There was always the twelve, often Peter, James, and John went and were taken further, and finally you have John the Beloved, the Revelator (the one who loved Jesus, always hanging on to Him, probably teased some by the other apostles, however he wrote the last book of the canon of the scriptures, Revelation, which is the unveiling of Jesus

Christ. See **Revelation 1:1**, "The Revelation of Jesus Christ…"

A final thought, it is quite interesting after Jesus speaks of covenant with the seventy and the twelve, and talks about their pursuit, the costs, then, after their hearts/soil is revealed, they leave. Have you ever noticed, this is recorded in John 666 (left colon out on purpose), Selah!

Pursuit

Pursuit defines simply as, "the action of following or pursuing someone or something." Some synonyms are, "chasing, shadowing, seeking, **going all out**, inquiring, hunting."

In Matthew's gospel, Jesus approaches four men whose occupation was fishermen. They were the ones experienced in "throwing the nets" and here comes the Lord and what does he do? He cast a spiritual net (calling) in their direction, then waited for their response. What they did, how they responded would today be, at best, very uncommon. They left "their nets" and picked up his! No debate, no fasting and praying for days on end, not needing confirmation, they followed.

Matthew 4:18-22

Your Pursuit Will Cost You (and reveal where you are)

Matthew 19:16-25

In essence, this rich young ruler was questioning Jesus as to what it was going to take, what was it going to cost him to pursue him, to receive what he was offering, eternal life. I tend to think Jesus first response to the man's question was entry-level, to reel him in so to speak. Jesus wanted to reveal the heart/soil condition that for all intents and purposes would hinder the ruler's request.

Jesus said, "just keep the commandments, don't commit adultery, don't shed innocent blood, don't steal, don't be an untrue testifier (don't offer what is false as true), honor your parents, and finally, love (agape) your fellowman, care for and be concerned for them as you are yourself."

Can you imagine the sigh of relief? "Well Master, I have done all this since I was very young, am I still falling short in something, is there something that will take me out of the race and potentially hinder me from reaching the goal?"

At this point Jesus deals with the heart issue, with the man's soil:

Matthew 19:21-22 (DHP)

My personal belief is that **his possessions owned him, he did not own his possessions**. He did not understand the kingdom's principle of sowing and reaping, giving, and receiving, seed, time, and harvest. His action, going back, revealed his heart and soil. One other thought (mine), I am not totally convinced Jesus would have **required him to sell all, but he had to been willing to**. Remember, even the Apostle Paul referenced writing to the Corinthian church (**1 Corinthians 13:3**), and teaching what we call the love chapter. He stated we could give all our goods (possessions, wealth, and properties) to the poor and still struggle operating in the agape of God (Selah)!

Matthew quoted Jesus in his writings and said:

Matthew 15:8 (KJV & DHP)

The Greek word for heart is *"kardia"* (pronounced: kar-dee-ah) and defines as, "denoting the center (seat) of all physical and spiritual life."

Jesus was stating there are certain people who say the right things (that can be heard and seen externally) yet the problem, the issue, the deception is internally, in the heart, the unseen realm, the soil if you will (my thoughts).

Hosea, one of the minor prophets in the Old Testament penned these words during a certain season with God's people, "they were destroyed (Hebrew-failed, perished, to become undone) because they rejected (Hebrew-abhorred, despised, distained, loathed, refused) knowledge" (See **Hosea 4:6**). John's gospel unfolds again the concept of pursuit:

John 8:31-32

III) A SYNOPTIC LOOK AT THE GOSPELS OF THE PARABLE OF THE SOWER
LESSON 3

A Comparison of Matthew, Mark, Luke, & The Gospel According to Thomas (see articles and information below on the Gospel According to Thomas).

See the definition of the word **parable** in the beginning of chapter one. In a synopsis of the gospels, three of the four share the events and the teaching by Jesus of this parable. Much to my amazement and surprise, as I was researching the internet in writing this manuscript,

I found an original copy (first printed in 1959) of the "Gospel According To Thomas." No, it is not in the 66 books of what we refer to as the canon of scripture, yet there have been other manuscripts/writings found that were referenced yet were decided against being included.

HERE IS THE PARABLE AS RECORDED BY THOMAS:

The Gospel According to Thomas

Log 9 (page 7)

Whoever has ears to hear let him hear. **4** Jesus said: See, the Sower went out, he filled his hand and, he threw. Some (seeds) fell on the road; **6** the birds came, they gathered them. **Others fell on the rock and did not strike root, 8 in the earth** and did not produce ears. And others fell on the thorns; **10** they choked the seed and the worm ate them. And others fell on the good earth; **12** and it brought forth good fruit; it bore sixty per measure and one hundred twenty per measure (this is the exact wording as found in The Gospel According to Thomas, New York And Evanston, Harper & Row, Copyright, E. J. Brill, 1959).

The phrase in **Verse 7** caught my attention. The seed "fell on the rock and did not strike root in the earth." The primary root is called the "radicle," it is the first thing to emerge from the seed. This radicle anchors the plant to the ground (soil) and then it begins to absorb water, as the root absorbs the water, a shoot emerges from the seed planted.

The root that develops directly from the radicle is called the **"true root."** The root of the plant that develops from the radicle is the embryonic root which is located at the lower end of the embryonic axis or the primary root of the seed. The radicle is the first organ to emerge from the germinating seed and grows downwards into the soil, anchoring the seedling and absorbing water and nutrients from the soil. As the radicle grows and develops, it gives rise to lateral roots, which further expand the root system of the plant and facilitates the uptake of water and nutrients from the soil *(This paragraph was written by a college graduate from Osmania University, graduated 2020, who majored in Botany Cytogenetics, Molecular Genetics & Biotechnology on the Quora App).*[1]

As you can plainly see in the above stated paragraphs, the seed and the soil have very specific dynamics in order to work together for the desired result. Thomas stated that the rocky ground was the hindrance to the seed taking root. Again, the soil was the issue, not the seed. I believe that I am safe to say that the return, (fruit, harvest) is primarily based on the soil, not the seed.

Luke's Account:

Luke penned his account of the parable in **Luke 8:4-15**, we will only investigate **Verse 15**. I believe that my paraphrase will expand further the phrase in bold below.

15 But that on the good ground are they, which **in an honest and good heart, having heard the word, keep** *it,* **and bring forth fruit with patience**.

15 The good ground (excellent in its nature and characteristics, genuine and approved for harvest, and fertile) are those who possess an honorable, excellent, upright, and distinguished heart (the center and seat of all physical and spiritual life), they give audience and attention to what is being taught and announced, the logos (written-revealed) sayings, decrees, mandates, and sayings of God and His Kingdom, they don't just hear, they hold fast, they take firm possession of what they

heard, and because their soil (heart) is fertile, they are fruitful and patient even in the fruits development and process, remaining steadfast, consistent, even cheerfully enduring knowing it is coming. (DHP)

Matthew's Account:

Matthew wrote concerning this parable in **Matthew 13:1-23**. We will examine **Verses 5-6**.

5 Some fell upon stony places, where they had not much earth: and forthwith they sprung up, because they had no deepness of earth:

> **5** Part of the seed descended upon rocky surfaces, in this place, there were more rocks than soil (earth which is necessary), at once, almost immediately a shoot appeared above the ground, but the fruits potential was denied as there was no depth (abundance) of the proper soil. (DHP)

The Preachers Homiletical Commentary says, "not soil containing loose stones, but a bed of rock, with only a slight covering of soil."

6 And when the sun was up, they were scorched; and because they had no root, they withered away.

> **6** Then, when the heat escalated because the rays of the sun increased, the torture (the trial, persecution, and tribulation) from the heat burned up what had sprung up, there was no depth of root as a result of no depth of soil, it's potential harvest dried up as the consequence of the

shallowness of the soil and the absence of moisture (water). (DHP)

Mark's Account:

Mark wrote his account of this in **Mark 4:1-20**. We will examine **Verses 2, 5, 7, 8, 13, and 15**.

2 And he taught them many things by parables, and said unto them in his **doctrine,**

> **2** He imparted instruction (expounded doctrine) often (frequently) in parables revealing the duties of men and the things of God, many times dealing with the nature and history of God's kingdom. He would tell earthly stories that carried heavenly meanings. (DHP)

5 And some fell on stony ground, where it had not much earth; and immediately it **sprang up, because it had no depth of earth**:

> **5** Other seed fell on ground dominated by rocks (the hinderance to growth and lasting fruit) with little or no soil (earth), almost immediately, you could see the beginning of a shoot coming up out of the rocky ground, the rock hindered the seed from reaching a depth in the soil (earth), to develop a deep and strong root system to sustain the seed during germination, development, growth and eventually harvest. (DHP)

7 And some fell among thorns, and the thorns grew up, and **choked it, and it yielded no fruit.**

7 Some seed the Sower released landed in thorny plants, briar bushes (woody thorns, prickly stems), as the thorns continued to grow, to spring up, in the end, they completely strangled the seed sown to the point that the seed yielded no benefit, advantage, profit or fruit. (DHP)

8 And other fell on good ground, and did yield fruit that sprang up and **increased**; and brought forth, some thirty, and some sixty, and some an hundred.

8 Finally, some seed fell (alighting) on excellent (in its nature) choice soil, the right soil released the seeds potential, rising up out of the earth (the unseen realm) into the visible (the external), this increase enabled what was hidden to be seen by all, it yielded 30-fold, 60-fold, up to 100-fold (God's choicest and best). (DHP)

My challenge here is simple, why settle for 30-fold when 60-fold is available, why settle for 60-fold when 100-fold is available? Why settle for the good or the acceptable when the perfect will of God is available? (See **Romans 12:2.**) Why settle for the outer court (30-fold), when the Holy Place is available (60-fold), why settle for the Holy Place (60-fold) when the Holy of Holies (Most Holy Place, 100-fold) is available? Selah (think on this)! Allow the seed to complete its process.

13 And he said unto them, **Know** ye not this parable? and how then will ye **know** all parables?

I will do my **DHP** of this verse here but will go into deeper study later in the book.

13 As he continued speaking with them, he stated with the utmost importance of knowing, perceiving and understanding this doctrine and its precepts (the general rule intended to regulate behavior and thought) that he was making known, then he declared, you will struggle to understand/comprehend another other parable that I teach in the days to come. (DHP)

The word "**know**" is used two times in this verse in the KJV, however, there are two different Greek words used. The first "**know**" is the Greek word "*eido*" (pronounced "i-do) and references, "perceiving, discerning, discovering with the mind, to inspect and examine, to pay attention to." The second word "**know**" is the Greek word "*ginosko*" (pronounced: ghin-oce-ko) and defines as, "to become acquainted with, to have knowledge." However, the last definition really caught my attention. It is a Jewish idiom for sexual intercourse between a man and a woman. I believe Jesus was letting His disciples know that if they did not get this revelation, this doctrine, truth (parable), if they did not understand that this one was foundational to the understanding and the unveiling of all the other parables that He would speak.

15 And these are they by the wayside, where the word is sown; but **when they have heard, Satan cometh immediately**, and **taketh away the word that was sown in their hearts**.

In Mark's account, once they had Jesus alone, they ask Him to explain/expound on the parable He had spoken to the multitude, in **Verse 15**, He proceeds sharing from His teaching earlier in the day.

15 Those journeying the well-traveled road (stop just long enough to casually or accidentally hear the message (the seed that was sown, the sayings of God), then, as soon as they hear the instruction, doctrine, and teaching, immediately God's adversary, the enemy, satan comes on the scene to make them doubt in order to remove that which was committed to them, he does not want it to become the center (seat) of their physical and spiritual life. (DHP)

The purpose of this chapter was for us to see and further understand the synoptic gospels versions/writings by His disciples (apostles) on the most important of all parables according to Jesus.

In the rest of this manuscript, we will look primarily at Matthew's gospel (version) of this kingdom parable.

---

1. Gorvadhan Ch, "Msc Botany in Cytogenetics, Molecular Genetics & Biotechnology (college major), Osmania University (Graduated 2020)," Quora, accessed February 24, 2024, https://qr.ae/psT8JL.

IV) THE PROBLEM IS NOT THE SEED

LESSON 4

1 Peter 1:23

Being born again, not of corruptible seed, but of incorruptible, by the word of God, which liveth and abideth forever.

> **23** Being born anew will reveal a new kingdom mindset, as you walk this out, it will conform you to walk in/and according to God's will, now living the God life (*zoe*), the seed that produced this new life has no corruption in it, none what soever, it cannot perish, wither, spoil, become defiled, or come to ruin. This seed is the sayings, decrees, and mandates given/spoken by God himself, his personal discourse, instruction, and doctrine. This seed is active, endless, full of life (His), and will continue and last forever, it has no end, it is eternal. (DHP)

The entirety of God creating in the book of beginnings, Genesis (the origin or mode of formation of something) was three-fold, essentially, He **spoke, He made/created, and** He **seeded** (planted). Notice in **Genesis 1**.

He spoke:

3 And God said,

5 And God called (Hebrew "*qara*" pronounced: kaw-raw, which defines as, "to address by name").

Verses 6,8,9,10, "and God called",11,14,20,24,26,29, "And God said…"

He made/created:

16 And God made (Hebrew "*asah*" pronounced: aw-saw, it means to produce, to press, to squeeze, fashion, and work).

Verse 21 And God created.

Verse 25 And God made.

Verse 27 So God created.

He seeded/planted:

Look at **Genesis 2**.

8 And the LORD God planted (Hebrew "*nata*" pronounced: naw-tah, it translates as, to establish by planting).

1:11 Let the earth bring forth grass, the herb yielding seed, *and* the fruit tree yielding fruit after his kind, whose **seed** *is* **in itself**.

1:12 And the earth brought forth grass, *and* herb **yielding seed after his kind**, and the tree yielding fruit, whose **seed** *was* **in itself**.

The Hebrew word for seed is *"zera"* pronounced: zeh-rah, it gives the idea of sowing, then, to bear, conceive, and offspring.

THE CLIMAX:

Genesis 1:31

31 And God saw.

In **Genesis 3:15**, God (himself) speaks the first prophecy continuing the seed concept. Eve was deceived (**1 Timothy 2:14**) as the serpent beguiled (Hebrew: seduced, led her astray) her. Adam's action was willful disobedience, then God declared:

15 And I will put enmity between thee and the woman, and between thy seed and her seed; it shall bruise thy head, and thou shalt bruise his heel.

> **15** From this day forward, hatred, hostility and enmity (a deep-rooted hatred) will be seen between you satan and what you manifest, the woman and what she conceives and produces, what comes from/through her will crush what you have now taken the headship of, her offspring will regain what you through your deception has stolen, the only thing noticeable on them will be a bruised heel from walking on you. (DHP)

There are some powerful hidden gems in this prophecy. God speaks of the seed of the woman; however, the woman has no seed, she has a womb, the man has the seed. There was a seed coming through a woman (Mary) who had not known a man intimately, if it was a natural birth and Joseph was the biological father, redemption would have not been available. The seed prophesied was Jesus, the Christ, and through his sinless life and nature, he would fulfill the prophecy by crushing the head of satan, and restoring man back to God's original intent, he would gain headship back that the enemy had stolen.

If I may be so bold, God sowed his Son (seed) into the earth, remember (**John 3:16**), God so loved the world (Greek "*kosmos*" which defines as, "universe, the earth and its inhabitants") that He gave (Greek "*didomi*" pronounced: did-o-mee, which speaks of suppling, furnishing, presenting, and to commission). Gave who? Christ! God's love, not his wrath is the source of redemption for mankind. Paul, the Apostle expounded on this truth to the Corinthian church:

2 Corinthians 9:15

Thanks *be* unto God for his unspeakable gift.

The word unspeakable better translates as, "indescribable, inexpressible."

After the creation spoken of in Genesis, chapters one and two, God sets forth the seed principle throughout the scriptures. **Genesis 8:22** reminds us of this truth. The first phrase establishes the duration, then the principle (in ***bold italics*** for emphasis).

22 *While the earth remaineth*, seedtime and harvest, and cold and heat, and summer and winter, and day and night shall not cease.

22 As long as the earth (ground, soil) continues, there is/will be sowing time (planting), then what is sown will be harvested (reaped), cool then hot, summer with its fruit then the harvest, morning (day) and night, these will not end, desist, or stop. (DHP)

The seed prophecy of **Genesis 3:15** is found again in the New Testament, in **Galatians 3:16,19,29**. Paul writing to the Galatian church affirms the prophecy spoken by God in the garden and reveals "who" the seed is and "who" is the offspring of that seed.

Who is the seed?

16 Now to Abraham and his seed were the promises made. He saith not, And to seeds, as of many; but as of one, And to thy seed, which is **Christ**.

16 The promised announcement which was a divine assurance of good (blessing) was made to Abraham and his seed (the future, which was yet in his loins, would ultimately reveal a family, tribe, and nation). What was prophesied and coming would be released through one seed (not many), and the seed had/has a name, Christ, yet the one seed, Christ, would produce a holy nation, why? Because the seed itself was/is holy. (DHP)

19 Wherefore then *serveth* the law? It was added because of transgressions, **till the seed should come** to whom the promise was made; *and it was* ordained by angels in the hand of a mediator.

19 So why do you continue as a slave operating under the law, it preceded the prophesied coming seed (Christ), it was added as the result of Adam's sin which released his fallen nature to all of humanity (the law, its effect, and it consequences were made manifest until Christ fulfilled/abolished it, see **Matthew 5:17, Romans 10:4, 2 Corinthians 3:11, Ephesians 2:14-16**), The promised seed came, fulfilled the prophecy, fulfilled the law, then abolished it (the law was a continual reminder that man was in a sinful state since Adam and needed a savior, a deliverer, and a redeemer). (DHP)

One other interesting point, in the Apostle Paul's letter to the Corinthian church, he referred to the law as the "ministry of death" (see **2 Corinthians 3:6,7,9**).

29 And if ye *be* Christ's, then are ye Abraham's seed, and heirs according to the promise.

29 Now that you are in Christ, the anointed one, God's only begotten son (**John 3:16**) which differs from Adam, a created son (**Genesis 1:27, Luke 3:38**), and since you came through Abraham's linage, making you a descendant of his, the prophecy and the promise spoken over/to him includes you, thus making you an heir by right of sonship. (DHP)

The Greek word for begotten is "*monogenēs*" pronounced: mon-og-en-ace, it comes from two Greek words, G3441 and G1096 (Strongs); which means, *only born*, that is, *sole:* - only (begotten, child). The understanding is this, Adam was a created son, he didn't come through natural birth, God, himself created and formed him. On the other hand, Jesus was the only Son born of God. He did come through Mary's womb. She gave Him a body, but God gave Him His blood (which was perfect, sinless, not like that of Adam's after the fall).

Because of His sinless life, His death, burial, and resurrection, the grave could not hold nor keep Him. Why? He was the incorruptible seed spoken of earlier in this chapter. Now because of redemption through Christ, sonship was made available once again to all who would receive Him (the seed) and now many sons can be restored to God's original intent, a glorious son **(Hebrews 2:10)**. Now a new creation has come back into existence, and where is Christ (the seed) in correlation to this new man? Once more this new image man manifests the nature, character, and integrity that can only be revealed through the seed's origin (Christ).

Where is the seed?

If you enjoy a good mystery movie, you watch it intently looking for any/all clues that would bring to light "whodunnit," after the revealing, it is no longer a mystery because the mystery had been solved.

Colossians 1:26-27

26 *Even* **the mystery which hath been hid from ages** and from generations, **but now is made manifest** to his saints:

27 To whom God would make known what *is* the riches of the glory of this mystery among the Gentiles; which is **Christ in you**, the hope of glory:

26 The mystery (the thing which had been hidden, concealed), the very purpose and counsel of God which had been kept secret from nations and the world, but now, at this moment, it is being disclosed (made known) to all of those committed and consecrated to him. (DHP)

27 God having pre-determined to release this revelation (at the appointed time, see **Galatians 4:4-5**), this abundant wealth which flowed from God through Christ, the very splendor, glory, and magnificence which had been hidden from humanity (including satan himself) was now made available to every tribe, people group and nation. Are you ready for it? Here it is! It is Christ, our Messiah, and his anointing (given to him from the Father), all of this is now **IN** you, his new creation man, in seed form, waiting to be developed, grown, pruned, watered, and fertilized to reveal Christ through you in the same manner that He revealed the Father through himself, his son. (DHP)

SOME FINAL THOUGHTS AS WE CLOSE OUT THIS CHAPTER.

Jesus spoke some powerful thoughts (actually, referring to himself, his purpose and mission) in John's gospel:

John 12:24

24 Verily, verily, I say unto you, Except a corn of wheat fall into the ground and die, it abideth alone: but if it die, it bringeth forth much fruit.

24 From this very truth I speak to you, unless a grain (a kernel of seed) falls (descends from a higher place to a lower place) and is planted, buried into the earth (ground) and dies, until it dies, the one seed remains alone, without offspring, then at death, something incredible and amazing happens, literally a miracle. The seed (grain) that died, and then out of death brings forth and produces life, great in multitude, in quantity. (DHP)

NOTES FROM ADAM CLARKE'S COMMENTARY:

Except a corn of wheat fall into the ground and die - Our Lord compares himself to a grain of wheat; his death, to a grain sown and decomposed in the ground; his resurrection, to the blade which springs up from the dead grain; which grain, thus dying, brings forth an abundance of fruit. I must die to be glorified; and, unless I am glorified, I cannot establish a glorious Church of Jews and Gentiles upon earth. In comparing himself thus to a grain of wheat, our Lord shows us: -

1. The cause of his death - the order of God, who had rated the redemption of the world at this price; as in nature he had attached the multiplication of the corn to the death or decomposition of the grain.

2. The end of his death - the redemption of a lost world; the justification, sanctification, and glorification of men: as the multiplication of the corn is the end for which the grain is sown and dies.

3. The mystery of his death, which we must credit without being able fully to comprehend, as we believe the dead grain multiplies

itself, and we are nourished by that multiplication, without being able to comprehend how it is done.

There is another side to the seed concept, all seeds are not good, weeds are also seeds. Recently I was speaking at a yearly conference in Texas with a dear friend of mine, Apostle Anthony Turner, and he made this statement that truly spoke to me, and I believe it will you also. He said, "if you don't deal with it as a seed, one day you will have to deal with it as a tree."

————

A few more final thoughts as we close out this message in the series. For a seed to ground into what its DNA declares it is, there are a few **musts** for this to happen. The soil it is sown into must have the proper **nutrients**, the right amount of **water**, **sunlight** (in our circles, we would call it SON-light, the right amount of **heat** (temperature), and final **room to grow** and **time to grow** (SELAH)!

Remember **Genesis 8:22**, Seed-Time-Harvest. (In the natural, the soil is the major source of the nutrients needed to grow and become a plant. The three main ingredients in the soil are nitrogen (N), phosphorus (P) and potassium (K). For the spiritual seed to grow and mature, there must be the initial planting, the process of dying (to one's self), plenty of water (Word of God), an ongoing intimate relationship with the Son (sun) and the right amount of heat (which is two-fold), first, to burn away anything that is not biblically nutrient based that could hinder the seeds growth and process, and secondly, to continue to aid the development of the seed into its designated DNA.

V) CONTINUING THOUGHTS ON THE SEED
LESSON 5

In Mark's account of the parable of the Sower, he states in **Mark 4:4b**, "and **the fowls of the air** came and devoured it up." Later that day, when the disciples had Jesus alone, they ask him to expound on the parable further. In **Verse 15**, he makes known and identifies who/what the fowl of the air is, "but when they have heard, **satan cometh immediately**, and taketh away the word that was sown in their hearts." **Luke's** account uses almost the exact wording in **Luke 8:5**, "and it was trodden down, and the fowls of the air devoured it."

The interesting note in Mark and Luke's writing is that the fowl came at once (right away) to devour the seed. The Greek word for devour is *"katesthiō"* (pronounced: kat-es-thee'-o" which uses words/phrases like, "to strip one of his goods, to ruin by infliction and injury, to consume, to make a prey of." As Jesus responds to the disciple's request, he reveals the identity of the fowl in **Verse 15**, satan and he comes immediately!

Notes from John Gill's Commentary on **Mark 4:4**:

"and the fowls of the air came and devoured it up; the devils, who have their abode in the air, especially the prince of the posse of them; and the Syriac version reads it in the singular number, "and the fowl came"; that ravenous bird of prey, Satan, who goes about seeking what he may devour; and for this purpose attends where the word is preached, to hinder its usefulness as much as in him lies."

The Greek word for **satan** is "*satanas*" (pronounced: sat-an-as') and describes him as, "an adversary (one who opposes another in purpose or act), the inveterate adversary of God and Christ, circumventing men by his wiles, the accuser, the devil." The Greek word for **immediately** is "*eutheōs*" (pronounced: yoo-theh'-oce), it references something that happens, "at once, straight way, instantly." If he is the adversary of God and Christ as defined above, then he is also the ecclesia's adversary, the CHRIST-ones made in his image and likeness, those once again reflecting the Father and the Son as Adam did before his fall. Not only does the enemy want to hinder you from **"hearing"** the seed (Word), but his plan is also to stop the seed from being **"received"** in the correct soil, so the root process never occurs.

———

When a seed is exposed to the proper conditions, water and oxygen are taken in through the seed coat. The embryo's cell starts to enlarge. Then, the seed coat breaks open and the root emerges (downward-my thoughts) first, followed by the shoot (upward-my thoughts) that contains the leaves and the stem.

Sunlight (illumination, revelation, impartation-my thoughts) supports the germination process by warming the soil.[1]

I believe the **Genesis 3:15** prophecy from God himself of the coming seed who would conquer satan and restore what he had stolen, sonship with all its privileges, and bring man back to God's original intent and purpose. This profound declaration immediately after Adam's fall can be found in two key passages of scripture in the New Testament (not necessarily in chronological order).

REFERENCE #1

Matthew 16:13-20

While entering the coasts of Caesarea Philippi, Jesus asks his disciples a question. "Who do men say that I the Son of man am?" I am not necessarily convinced that Jesus was greatly concerned about what others were saying concerning himself. I believe he used the first question to get to the real question. "Whom say ye that I am?"

Simon Peter's answer was profound on many levels, first, as we look at the life of Peter, he often had a way of opening his mouth, inserting his foot, and chewing, as they say, eating your own words. In this dialogue with Jesus, it shows both sides of his two names (natures), Simon (reed) and Peter (a rock or stone). In his first statement in this passage, Peter makes known a previously unknown (mystery), revealing a long-time hidden truth that would be brought to the light that very day, in his second statement, Simon works through him again, then Jesus rebukes him and called him satan. If we are totally honest with ourselves, we have all been guilty of speaking out of both sides of our mouth on more than one occasion.

Peter answers Jesus's question in **verse 16**, "And Simon Peter answered and said, Thou art **the Christ, the Son of the living God**."

You are the anointed Messiah, the Son of the one and only true and living God, He is superior and carries the pre-eminence, there is none like him nor above him (You are the revealed **Genesis 3:15** seed of promise, **DHP**).

This was the first time this name was revealed and used in the New Testament and never used in the Old Testament. At the climax of that prophecy being released through Peter, Jesus states with resounding applause, "Peter, you did not get this through the flesh and blood doctrines and traditions of men, this came from the highest source and voice there is, my father laid open and uncovered what had been covered and veiled since the garden, showing you my true identity and purpose, the **Genesis 3:15** seed (my thoughts)."

Now, here is why I believe this is true and it fits in line with other scriptures and principles. In the beginning of this chapter, we looked in-depth at the words, **satan** and **immediately**. The concept is in the quickness of the enemy coming in to steal the seed, truth, and revelation that was made known. Why? Before the seed, truth and revelation can take root.

After Peter receives and reveals this truth, Jesus expounds on it in **verses 18-19 (DHP), see my paraphrase verses in Chapter 5**:

After Peter's revealing of the promised seed, the Christ, Jesus begins to unfold what he must go through to accomplish and fulfill the prophecy, but he also tells them, you now know this, however, it is not yet time to disclose it to others yet. He goes on to talk about the upcoming events, Jerusalem, the coming confrontation of the religious system of the day, the priests, elders, and scribes which will ultimately meet with his death, the crucifixion (which would fulfill **Genesis, 3:15, John 1:29, Revelation 13:8**).

Remember, once the seed is sown, its DNA, purpose, and potential destiny are revealed. That is why satan comes immediately, and it was no different on that day when Peter received the revelation. Notice his response to Jesus disclosing His purpose, and what He must go through to fulfill it:

Matthew 16:21-23 (DHP, see my paraphrases in Chapter 5)

REFERENCE #2

Matthew 3:13,16,17

13 Then cometh Jesus from Galilee to Jordan unto John, to be baptized of him.

16 And Jesus, when he was baptized, went up straightway out of the water: and, lo, **the heavens were opened** unto him, and he saw **the Spirit of God descending** like a dove, and lighting upon him:

17 And lo **a voice from heaven, saying, This is my beloved Son**, in whom I am well pleased.

John is baptizing Jesus in the Jordan river, from 12 years of age until now (30 years of age) it seems as if Jesus lived in obscurity as nothing is really recorded in the gospels, yet we know accordingly to Luke's account that he "grew in wisdom, stature, and favor with God and man" (**Luke 2:52**). He was growing, going through His own process, preparation, and development for the 3.5 years of ministry that was in front of Him.

As Jesus was coming up out of the waters of baptism, the heavens open, the Holy Spirit descends upon Him and the voice of the Father speaks, "this is My beloved Son." I believe in light of what we have penned so far which came through study, preparing the notes for this manuscript, and divine inspiration by the Holy Spirit, this is another reference (announcement) of the one who would fulfill the prophecy of **Genesis 3:15**.

On a side note, a thought to consider for those who may not be students of the Word (studiers). Jesus's public ministry began at baptism (age 30), yet there are no references or occurrences recorded in the gospels of Him performing one miracle before this day. Why? I believe the answer in found in the scriptures:

#1

"the Spirit of God descending like a dove, and lighting upon him" (**Matthew 3:16b**). There is no reference before here of the Holy Spirit being on Jesus or working with/through him.

This was the third person of the Trinity, descending upon him in the form of a dove, The dove, among the Jews, was the symbol of purity of heart, harmlessness, and gentleness, compare, **Psalm_55:6-7**. The form chosen here was doubtless an emblem of the innocence, meekness, and tenderness of the Saviour. The gift of the Holy Spirit, in this manner, was the public approbation of Jesus, **John 1:33**, and a sign of his being set apart to the office of the Messiah. We are not to suppose that there was any change done in the moral character of Jesus, but only that he was publicly set apart to his work, and solemnly approved by God in the office to which he was appointed (Albert Barnes commentary).

The Holy Spirit is the oil, the anointing. Jesus had to be anointed to do the greater works, signs, wonders, and miracles. As you read this, you may be saying NO! But wait, there is more. Another verse some may have never read or need to be reminded of.

#2

Acts 10:38

How **God anointed Jesus of Nazareth with the Holy Ghost** and with power: who went about doing good, and healing all that were oppressed of the devil; for God was with him.

> **38** God the father, the first person of the trinity, consecrated Jesus to his Messianic assignment, furnishing him with the necessary powers for its administration, the Holy Ghost (Spirit), releasing his strength, power, and ability to him and to operate through him. His journey of public ministry for the next 3.5 years had begun, he did good, bestowing benefits (Greek meaning-philanthropic, one who seeks to promote the welfare of others, giving generously to good causes) on the people, bringing them

the gift of salvation, healing them, applying the cure for sin and the curse, making them whole, setting free the oppressed, those under the control and exploited by the enemy, God now working with/through him. (DHP)

ANOTHER PROOF:

Matthew 4:1

1 Then was Jesus **led up of the Spirit** into the wilderness to be tempted of the devil.

To be led by the Spirit, he had to be endowed with the Spirit. God announced in **Matthew 3:17**, Jesus was His Son (the seed prophesied in **Genesis 3:15**). He was now empowered to do, fulfill, and accomplish the will of His Father. This may challenge our thinking some but according to **verse one**, God did the leading through the Holy Spirit, the devil did the tempting.

The phrase, "**led up**" in the Greek describes one who navigates from a lower place to a higher place. The Holy Spirit would lead/navigate/be with him through the temptation. The Greek word for tempted is "*peirazō*" (pronounced: pi-rad'-zo) which translates as, "to test, to scrutinize, to entice, to examine, to test for the purpose of finding out one's qualities, what they think, how they behave themselves, and finally their faith and character."

What God had just declared over Him would be immediately tested. Remember, how quickly the enemy comes to steal/challenge the seed? Immediately! An interesting thought, in Matthew's gospel (**Matthew 4:1-3**) and Luke's gospel (**Luke 4:1-3**), that the devil came and began the temptation after the forty days, not during the forty days. After forty days of fasting (dealing with the flesh), and prayer (intimacy with the Father), the devil decides to show up. In my opinion, he was forty days late. Notice the enemy's question during the day of testing? It was the same question.

Matthew 4:3

"If thou be the Son of God…"

Matthew 4:6

"If thou be the Son of God…"

In light of this manuscript and taking two complete chapters to reveal the **Genesis 3:15** seed prophecy, I am convinced throughout the Bible's history, satan **DID NOT** know that Jesus was the fulfillment of that prophetic word. Why? Even in many books of the Old Testament, there are examples of the enemy causing death, darkness, evil and corruption, but the prophecy made it through. The enemy was wondering, pondering, was it Noah (**Genesis 6:1**)? Was it Moses (**Exodus 1:22**)? Was it David, Gideon, Samson, or another?

Each time the seed (promise) made it through, for it was for a yet appointed time. When Peter revealed the Christ and God revealed His Son (seed), it was no longer a mystery. Peter revealed it, Simon tried to talk Jesus out of it. God announced it, satan came immediately to question, to conquer, to see that the seed never got planted, or at best, uprooted. But God's prophecy would come to pass, the Lamb would literally be slain (as it always had happened in the mind of God before He framed the world). The seed Jesus would be planted, die, and resurrection just like the seeds designed DNA. Remember these verses:

1 Corinthians 2:7-8

7 But we speak the wisdom of God in a mystery, *even* the hidden *wisdom,* which God ordained before the world unto our glory:

8 Which none of the princes of this world knew: for had they known *it,* they would not have crucified the Lord of glory.

God's enemy fell right into His plan and had no discernment as to the outcome. Each time satan asked the question, "if you be the Son of God?" I believe he had a two-fold purpose, he wanted to know, and he wanted Jesus to question it.

————

A final thought in closing, the last statement in the temptation was an offer from the devil, look closely:

Matthew 4:8-9

8 Again, the devil taketh him up into an exceeding high mountain, and **sheweth him all the kingdoms of the world, and the glory of them;**

9 **And saith unto him, All these things will I give thee**, if thou wilt fall down and worship me.

Jesus **did not** question or challenge if the kingdoms belonged to him, at that moment, they were still under his control from the fall of Adam. They had to be his or it would not have been a legitimate temptation. Selah! The truth was if Jesus had given in and worshiped him, he would have not given them to Him, and mankind would have been doomed for eternity.

Jesus's answer was:

Matthew 4:10

10 Then saith Jesus unto him, Get thee hence, Satan: for it is written, Thou shalt worship the Lord thy God, and him only shalt thou serve.

Luke's account states that the devil departed the failed temptation for a **"season"** (**Luke 4:13**). If the enemy came at Jesus, the seed, more than once, rest assured, he will come at you to question, challenge the prophetic words spoken over you which are tied to your purpose and destiny, he will try and cause you to doubt, his plan never changed, he wants to steal the seed, kill its purpose and destroy its destiny.

> I declare over you right now, I prophesy that your latter shall be greater than your former, your seed is tied to your calling and has a kingdom purpose, it will not be uprooted. The eyes of your understanding are gaining new enlightenment at this very moment, your past will not dictate your future, better is the end of a thing than the beginning, it is not how you start, it is how you finish, and you will finish strong, you will finish your race, you will cross the finish line, you will get a winner's wreath. Your tears will turn into laughter, your sorrow into joy, your failures into victories, your best is yet to come. It is NOT over, God, not satan, has the last word.

———

Some final thoughts as we close out this chapter. In the Apostle Paul's letter to the Church in Ephesus, he continues to expound to another church the mystery, the revealing to His ekklesia, the manifold wisdom of God concerning the purpose of Christ, the prophesied seed once again in **Genesis 3:15**. The evidence is unarguable, undeniable, unquestionable, and undisputable throughout the scriptures that the prophesy was/is fulfilled.

Ephesians 3:9-11

9 And to make all *men* see what *is* the fellowship of the mystery, which from the beginning of the world hath been hid in God, who created all things by Jesus Christ:

10 To the intent that now unto the principalities and powers in heavenly *places* might be known by the church the manifold wisdom of God,

11 According to the eternal purpose which he purposed in Christ Jesus our Lord:

Also see **Verses 9-11** from my paraphrase (DHP) in **Chapter 5**.

Consider this: Jesus left the planet, Christ **NEVER** did!

I have a two-volume set called, *Weekly Word Studies With the Doc*. It contains one hundred words and phrases in the Old & New Testaments. It is designed to study one per week (not like the traditional daily devotional). In volume one, week 22, I wrote on the word, "**seed**." You can order one or both volumes through our ministry.

---

1. Mary Beth Bennett, "Germinating Seeds," WVU Extension Service (February 1, 2021), accessed February 24, 2024, https://extension.wvu.edu/lawn-gardening-pests/news/2021/02/01/germinating-seeds#:~:text=When%20a%20seed%20is%20exposed,process%20by%20warming%20the%20soil.

VI) THE PARABLE OF THE SOWER
LESSON 6

In the first five lessons, we uprooted some wrong mindsets, misconceptions, and even bad foundations that were poured from the traditions of men and religious systems that are void of the kingdom message being revealed and released into the earth.

Jesus taught many parables throughout His earthly time of ministry, only twelve of them started with the phrase, "the kingdom of heaven is like." This parable is the only one of the kingdom parables where Jesus made this profound statement in Mark's gospel.

Mark 4:13

13 And he said unto them, **Know ye not this parable? and how then will ye know all parables**?

> 13 Jesus spoke to his disciples and said, "If you do not perceive, discern, inspect and examine this kingdom

parable (this earthly story with a heavenly meaning), if you do not become acquainted with this parable intimately to the point of knowing and understanding it, as it is foundational, by what means will you be able to understand the other parables which I will reveal?" (DHP)

The Parable of the Sower & the Seed

In Matthew's gospel, he pens his version of the Sower Parable, we find Jesus sitting by the seaside, a great multitude gathers around Him, then He steps into a ship, sits down, and begins His discourse on this kingdom parable.

Matthew 13:3-9 (See my paraphrase verses in Chapter 6)

Some seeds fell by the way-side - That is, the hard "path" or headland, which the plow had not touched, and where there was no opportunity for it to sink into the earth (Albert Barnes Commentary).

It is important to know and understand that this parable is **NOT** about **four types of seed,** it is about **four types of soil**.

In this parable, I believe the Lord reveals and expounds on a major kingdom key to experience the fruit that is available to His sons and daughters, the importance of the soil.

THE PURPOSE OF PARABLES

His answer to them in Verse unveils a side of Him that many without study and research would seriously question.

Verses 10-12

The Greek word for **mysteries** is *"musterion"* (pronounced: moos-tay-ree-on), it describes a "hidden thing, religious secrets, confided only to the initiated and not to ordinary mortals, not obvious to the understanding, a hidden purpose or counsel of God: the secret counsels which govern God in dealing with the righteous, which are hidden from ungodly and wicked men but plain to the godly." (Thayer's)

Here is a challenge to all as we teach this series: The Kingdom message and its keys are revealed to the teachable, the hungry, those pursuing righteousness, **NOT** the average church attendee, who goes occasionally, never brings their Bible, let alone a notebook, often there for wrong motives, to pass out their business cards, to build their downline, to get free babysitting services, I think you get the point. Selah!!!

Notice the phrase in **Verse 12**, "whosoever hath." Hath what? Stay in the context of what Jesus was teaching. **He who has knowledge of the mysteries of the kingdom** (that answer is found in **Verse 11** above). He told His disciples that these kingdom keys were given to them to **KNOW**. The Greek word **know** is *"ginosko"* (pronounced: ghin-oce-sko) which translates as, "to perceive, to understand where you can speak," it is also a Jewish idiom for sexual intercourse between a man and a woman.

I believe that it takes this type of spiritual intimacy with God, His Word (Jesus) and His Spirit (Holy Spirit) to become intimate with these keys and truths. It will be a life-long endeavor on our part for these kingdom truths/secrets to be revealed, imparted into our lives, and lived out. The more we pursue Him, the more of Himself He reveals.

2 Timothy 2:15 (See my paraphrase of Verse 15 in Chapter 6)

The Greek word for **study** is "*spoudazo*" (pronounced: spoo-dad-zo) which defines as, "to be diligent, prompt or earnest to do, to exert oneself." Only this type of person can truly rightly divide, a studier (not a reader).

More insight into our responsibility:

John 8:31-32 (Also see DHP Verses)

The Greek word for **continue** is "*meno*" (pronounced: men-o) and it means, "to remain, abide, to sojourn, tarry, to not depart, to continue to be present, to be held, kept, to remain as one, not to become another or different."

I believe that **Verse 31** is the acid-test of our faith and trust in the Lord and His word. **John 14:21** acted upon with more than just words prove our commitment and faith. "He that hath my commandments, and keepeth them, he it is that loveth me: and he that loveth me shall be loved of my Father, and I will love him, and will **manifest** myself to him." I love the promise given here to those who "loves him with actions keeping his commandments (being a doer of the word)." His promise is, "I will manifest myself to those." The Greek word for **manifest** is "*emphanizō*" (pronounced em-fan-id'-zo) which defines as, "to appear, to exhibit (in person), to reveal."

James continues to expand on this truth of "hearing **and** doing" in his writings.

James 1:22-25 (also DHP Verses)

Back to the parable in Matthew's gospel:

Matthew 13:16-17

What did the disciples see and hear? The mysteries of the kingdom were revealed unto them. I trust that you realize how blessed you truly are and the potential you have inside of you when you attend a true ekklesia (church) that teaches the message Jesus taught. Jesus continues to disclose some interesting thoughts in **Verse 17**.

The Old Testament prophets and righteous men did not see or hear what? The revealing of the mysteries of the Kingdom that His disciples were experiencing firsthand. At best, they only knew about them in types and shadows of what was to come.

Another side note:

Luke 16:16

16 The law and the prophets *were* until John: since that time the kingdom of God is preached, and every man presseth into it.

16 The law and the prophets remained until John, since then, the good news about the Kingdom of God has been proclaimed, and everyone entering it is under attack. (International Standard Version)

The Pentateuch (Genesis-Deuteronomy) revealed the law, then Joshua through Malachi, the major and minor prophets referenced the coming of a King and His kingdom. These all heard and even proclaimed of a coming King and His Kingdom, but never saw or experienced what Jesus disciples and you and I have heard, seen, and experienced. I find it compelling that the

International Standard Version of **Verse 16** says, "everyone entering it is under attack."

In Luke's gospel, Jesus states that the message of the law and a coming kingdom through the prophets was preached until John (the Baptist). Wait!!! Until John, then He said that the message would change. Why? Because He, Jesus had come to fulfill the law since man could not, then reveal the Father's plan of the king, His kingdom, and their purpose. This message's greatest enemy is religion and the self-imposed traditions of men.

So, I continue to proclaim **many preach messages about Jesus**, but **not many preach the message Jesus preached**.

One more scriptural proof of preaching this message will bring attacks, from religious men often influenced by the "messenger of satan." The Apostle Paul was harassed because of the message he carried and preached, fulfilling his kingdom assignment.

2 Corinthians 12:7-10 (See DHP Verses)

———

An interesting side note on the phrase, "a thorn in the flesh." The Greek word for **thorn** is not found another time in the entire New Testament.

Because of the depth of information that we are pursuing, we will continue these thoughts in Lesson 7.

VII) THE PARABLE OF THE SOWER (PART 2)

As we continue teaching this kingdom parable that Jesus taught in **Matthew 13**, let us closely inspect the next several verses (**Verses 18-23**) in His teaching. Jesus began to explain (expand) the Parable of the Sower to His disciples after they questioned His reasoning for teaching in Parables.

Matthew 13:18-19 (See DHP also)

In John Gill's commentary, his notes on the phrase, "and understandeth it not" are extremely insightful:

"and understandeth it not with his heart. He is one that is careless and inattentive, negligent and forgetful; has some slight notions of things as he hears, but these pass away as they come; his affections are not at all touched, nor his judgment informed by them, but remains as stupid, and as unconcerned as ever; his heart is not opened to attend to, and receive the word, but continues hard and obdurate; and is like the common and beaten road, that is trodden down by everyone, and is not susceptible of the seed, that falls upon it." (John Gill)

"perhaps more properly, regardeth it not, does not lay his heart to it." (Adam Clarke)

When Jesus said, "and understandeth it not," what was He referencing? The answer is found in the first few words in **Verse 19**, "the word of the kingdom."

The word **understandeth** is the Greek word *"suniemi"* (pronounced: soon-ee-ay-mee) which references, "perceiving, to set or join together in mind."

At this point, once again He expounds to His disciples what He had shared with the multitude, emphasizing the soil types. All too often, people attending their local churches, attending conferences, revivals, and camp meetings are quick to blame the messenger, even the message, as to the lack of results in their life, the lack of evident fruit the leader spoke of, and the absence of kingdom benefits taught.

Seldom do they look internally, questioning the type or condition of their own soil (mind, heart) being the hinderance. In Jesus's exhortation of this kingdom parable of the Sower, the seed, and the soil, He associates the lack of production (the harvest of the seed sown) on the condition of the soil, **NOT** the Sower or the seed.

In any given corporate service, the potential is there for all four soils to be in the service. The following mathematical example may not be too popular, but here goes. Doing the math, if all four soils are in a service in equal portions, only about 25% of the congregations' soil is conducive to the 100-fold increase spoken of by Jesus in **Matthew 13:8**.

We will look more in-depth at the four different types of soil later in this book, but for now, here are the soil types and the scriptures where they are revealed:

1. **The Wayside Soil (Matthew 13:4,19)**
2. **The Stony Place Soil (Matthew 13:5,20-21)**
3. **The Thorny Soil (Matthew 13:7,22)**
4. **The Good Ground Soil (Matthew 13:8,23)**

I believe one of the biggest hinderances to the seed's potential return can be found in an often quoted, but seldom understood verse of scripture also in Matthew's gospel. God did not leave us in the dark as to what is important and a must priority for our lives. **He wants His priority to be our priority! The Kingdom must be first, everything else is second.**

Dr. Munroe once made this statement, *"Nothing is yours until you understand it."*[1] To walk in the kingdom, to use its keys, you first must come to an understanding of it through your pursuit and your study until it becomes a rhema revelation to you, then you can/will enjoy all its benefits.

Matthew 6:33 (see DHP)

Synonyms for the word **seek** are "pursue, investigate, explore, learn, go after, understand, consider, and desire." The Greek word **first** is *"proton"* which means, "first in time, place, rank, influence, honor, the chief or principal thing." In the simplest definition, **"first things first."**

Starting back in **Verse 25**, Jesus said, "**take no thought.**" If you read these verses in context all the way down into **Verse 34**, I believe what He was saying, and it is confirmed in the Greek translation of the phrase was, "these things should not consume your thoughts, feelings, emotions, time, or energy. These can be distractions to your purpose, calling, and destiny. Avoid any distraction that hinders your purpose."

The Greek word that makes up the phrase "**take no thought**" is "**merimnao**" (pronounced: mer-im-nah-o) and defines as, "do not be anxious, concern yourself with, occupy your thoughts with, or trouble yourself with cares." Another derivative of the word states, "through the idea of distraction."

Jesus then uses the analogy of being preoccupied and it results in **Verse 27**.

Matthew 6:27 (DHP also)

In **Verses 31-32 (See DHP)**, He explains in more detail these distractions:

In John Gill's commentary, he states that these repetitive expressions reveal a man of little faith.

Another thought as we continue: The enemy will increase his attacks when he knows you are getting close/closer to the answer, when the light is being turned on and your life is about to be forever changed. He also attacks those who sow these kingdom principles (seeds) into people, individually, and corporately.

This message must become a revelation, a rhema word to you. Do not try to operate in them until they are rooted and grounded in the correct soil. Allow Holy Spirit to reveal your present soil, then, allow Him to do His work in you to produce the right, productive soil, this will stop much heartache, disappointment, and discouragement.

There is a huge difference as we have referenced in this series between "**hearing**" and "**knowing**." Hearing a truth without it taking root, developing, and maturing in the proper soil, and folks trying to act on/apply it will cause damage to yourself and potentially others.

Let us look at this example in the scriptures:

Acts 19:8-16

There are a few things in the above passage of scripture that should be examined in light of what I wrote in the paragraphs preceding it.

- The Apostle Paul taught for three months in the synagogue in Ephesus (**Verse 8**). The King James uses the words "disputing" and "persuading." What did he teach? The Kingdom! The word **disputing** is the Greek word "*dialegomai*" (pronounced: dee-al-eg-om-ahee), and it translates as, "to discourse with, to converse, to discuss." The other definitions that grabbed my attention was this, "to think different within one's self, to mingle thought with thought." Paul was conversing with some disciples and people in the church in Ephesus, he was teaching the kingdom, which by the word disputing's meaning, was challenging them that they would have to think differently than they had thought in order to see and experience the kingdom. Then we have the word,

persuading. It is the Greek word, *"peitho"* (pronounced: pi-tho) which defines as, "to induce one by words to believe, to convince."

- He was challenging their beliefs with the message of the kingdom, He was stating that their thoughts would have to change to see, understand, and experience the revelation he was endeavoring to impart. Remember, "For as he thinketh in his heart, so is he…" (**Proverbs 23:7**) The word **heart** also translates as **soul,** which throughout this manuscript I have interchanged with the word **soil**. As your soul (soil) gives thought to the seed being sown, depending on the condition of your soil and which of the 4 types it is dictates the rejection of the seed, the return from the seed, or the lack thereof.

- Upon hearing the kingdom message, some became very obstinate, unyielding to the message, refusing to believe the truths Paul was revealing (I have often taught that unbelief is far more dangerous than doubt, as doubt is a lack of information, but unbelief is a decision. You cannot operate in unbelief until after you have heard, then reject it). Those that rejected it immediately tried to impact others addressing the messenger and the message with offensive language. Remember: In **Matthew 13,** the kingdom parable states how quickly the enemy comes to steal the seed (message) before it can take root, and sadly, often, he uses religious unlearned people. Paul took the disciples (he separated the wheat from the tares) into the school Tyrannus and continued to teach them. (**Verse 9**)

John Gill in his commentary on the phrase, "**he departed from them**" wrote this, "the hardened, unbelieving, and blaspheming Jews, as being unworthy of the means of grace; he went out of their synagogue, and no more entered there: and separated the disciples; from them, the twelve disciples he had laid his hands on, and others who in this space of time, the space of three months, had been converted under his ministry; these he formed into a separate Gospel church state, as well as engaged them to quit the company and conversation of these blasphemers, and no more attend with them in their synagogue, that so they might not be infected and corrupted by them; a separation from such who contradict and blaspheme the truths and ordinances of the Gospel, is justifiable."

- Paul stayed in Asia and Ephesus, the chief city in Asia, for two years teaching and training, until all of that region of Asia had heard the kingdom message. If you are a minister reading this, do not let opposition, or religious mindsets sidetrack your purpose or your message. Your purpose is to preach/teach the message, the message is the kingdom! (**Verse 10**)

- Jesus preached the kingdom for 3.5 years and countless, signs, wonders, and miracles accompanied his message. Preaching the right message brings the right manifestations, they are confirmations, confirming the message with signs following.

The Apostle Paul continues Jesus' message and look what happens: Paul's teaching produced remarkable, uncommon, unusual miracles, even to the point that handkerchiefs (Greek word *"soudarion"* pronounced: soo-dar-ee-on, meaning a cloth for wiping the perspiration from the face, a sweat cloth) and aprons (a linen covering that workman and servants were accustomed to wearing) taken from Paul which he used/wore, and placed them on the sick and possessed, the sick were healed and the possessed were delivered. (**Verses 11-12**)

Once again, the notes in John Gill's Commentary shed more light on this: "**So that from his body were brought unto the sick.**" The Ethiopic version renders it, "from the extremity", or "border of his garment"; and the Syriac version, "from the garments which were upon his body"; were brought and put upon the sick; that is, of the clothes which the apostle wore, some of them were taken and carried to sick persons, and used by them: particularly "handkerchiefs" or "aprons"; the former were such as he might use to wipe his face with, and remove sweat, or any filth from the body; and the latter, what he might wear as a mechanic, when working at his trade:

- The Seven Sons of Sceva. During that time there were a group of wandering self-proclaimed exorcists, professing to tell people's fortunes, claiming to cure diseases with charms and spells. Hummm? I wonder if they were a group of uncommitted, unsubmitted, back-slidden prophets… just a thought. Sceva (means "mind reader") was a certain chief priest in Ephesus who had seven sons that were the wandering group following in his footsteps.

Apparently, they heard Paul speak to and cast out spirits, so they took it upon themselves to attempt to operate in a kingdom key based on a phrase they heard Paul use, and a Name they had no understanding of or relationship with. "We restrain you in the name that Paul preaches (proclaims)." And what happened? Wait for it…the evil spirit said,

> "I know Jesus is the Son of God, I know he has the power to dispossess (deprive to stay) spirits, and Paul, I am acquainted with him being a servant of the most high God, but who or what are you? You definitely are not a disciple of Jesus nor a servant of God, but you are children of the devil, you have no power over us, but on the other hand, you are subject to us." (DHP)

What was the result? The evil spirit through the possessed man grabbed a hold of them, beat them, wounded them, and stripped them naked. (**Verses 13-16**)

- What was the result? The reverence of God hit Ephesus and Asia, Jesus was exalted and celebrated, true repentance swept the countryside, conviction caused them to act bringing their books which they used for magic, soothsaying, necromancy, conjuring spirits and burned them in front of all in Ephesus, which was worth an incredible amount of money. In the end the Word of God increased in the region and overcame everything. (**Verses 17-20**)

---

1. Munroe, Myles. "Nothing if Yours Until You Understand It." YouTube video, 0:15. February 24, 2022. https://www.youtube.com/shorts/2Q8yo2_9AsA.

VIII) THE WAY-SIDE SOIL
LESSON 8

All too often in churches on Sunday mornings, many in the congregation will critique (assess, evaluate) the minister and their message through the lens of their own perception, life, present situations, or even their past, Yet I find it extremely interesting in this kingdom parable in **Matthew 13**, the Sower (minister) assesses the soil in those he is sowing into.

Matthew 13:4,19 (DHP also)

The KJV uses the phrase in **Verses 4,19** to describe the first type of soil as, "**way side**." Way-side soil sketches the idea of a hard beaten path in which no plow had broken up the ground, so there was no real opportunity for the seed to sink into, then take root in the soil. This also represents a ground trampled on by men, then because of no real depth and openness as a plow had not touched it, the seed was easily exposed and because clearly accessible prey to the fowls of the air.

The concept of a "hard beaten path" communicates its present condition was something that had developed over time. I want to challenge you to consider some thoughts prophetically concerning this first type of soil. This hardened soil was the reason that the seed did not take root, develop, and grow.

———

Let's delve into some truths referencing these four different soils, as I am convinced recognizing which soil we have, and why, with the Holy Spirit's help will reveal which soil it is, remove the things that have produced the wrong type of soil, heal us, and change our soil to good fertile ground that will produce the 100-fold return on the seed as promised.

One of the above references states that the path had hardened because the plow had not been applied. One reference stated the "way side" soil could also represent private paths that the individual had taken (almost presenting the concept that these were areas no one was allowed to see or walk them through…my thoughts).

As a result of the soil's condition, people had trampled on this person's soil (mind) greatly hindering the potential outcome. So, in this individual's life, the seed was never correctly planted which gave easy access to be devoured by the seed's greatest enemy (satan).

This soil can also speak of a hearer that is inattentive, negligent, then because of their negligence, correct, proper understanding does not happen so their judgment is off, their affection (love) for the seed (word) wanes. This person is distracted (even in corporate worship), preoccupied (mostly with the cares of life, things that have no eternal outcome, or things that have nothing to do with the service), eventually becoming skeptical of the Sower (minister) and the message (seed). They are not those who readily receive God's Word. Look again at **James 1:21**. **(DHP also)**.

John Gill states in his commentary, **"and the fowls came and devoured them**." The other evangelists say, "the fowls of the air." The Vulgate Latin and Munster's Hebrew Gospel, and some copies; and mean the devils; so called, because their habitation is in the air; hence they are said to be "the power of the air": and because of their ravenous and devouring nature, their swiftness to do mischief, and their flocking in multitudes, where the word is preached, to hinder its usefulness, as fowls do, where seed is sowing. Satan, and his principalities, and powers, rove about in the air, come down on earth, and seek whom they may devour, and often mix themselves in religious assemblies, to do what mischief they can; see **Job 1:6**.[1] "Now there was a day when the sons of God came to present themselves before the LORD, and Satan came also among them."

Another reason for the wayside soil (hard beaten path) was that a plow had not touched it. I want to challenge us right here to think "outside of the box" for a moment.

Hosea 10:11b-12 (DHP also)

This truth is again revealed in the book of **Zechariah 14:17**:

17 And it shall be, *that* whoso will not come up of *all* the families of the earth unto Jerusalem to worship the King, the LORD of hosts, even upon them shall be no rain.

The equation is quite simple: No worship=No rain=No crops/harvest. Selah!

Judah is the Hebrew word "*Yehudah*" (pronounced: yeh-hoo-daw) which means, "praise." The phrase, "**break up the fallow ground**" is the Hebrew word, "*niyr*" (pronounced: neer) which translates as, "to freshly plow, to till."

The writer of Judges (some traditional views believe that the Prophet Samuel wrote it) makes these prophetic statements in his writings. After Joshua's death, Israel asks the Lord who was to go into battle against the Canaanites? The Lord's answered with, "Judah shall go up." **Up** is the Hebrew word, "*alah*" (pronounced: aw-law) and defines as, "to ascend up, to mount up, to come up (before God). Praise takes you to a higher realm, it brings you up into/before the presence of God.

Judges 1:1-2

This type of praise and worship before God will assure you of the conquest in the battles of life that you are facing. Once again, Israel asks who was to go up first in battle against Benjamin. The answer was the same.

Judges 20:18

Another interesting and I believe very revealing prophetic truth. Which one of the twelve tribes of Israel that were encamped around the tabernacle of Moses (the pattern that he built according to God's blueprints where His presence would tabernacle among His people) had direct immediate access into the door (the east entrance) of God's presence?

Numbers 2:3

Judah was camped directly in front of the east entrance of the Tabernacle. Also, that was the only entrance into it. Can you begin to see the prophetic significance? Praise and worship will bring you into the Father's presence. Why does the majority of the Ekklesia (church) start their corporate services with praise and worship? Because it is groundbreaking, it plows, tills, loosens the soil (mind, heart), it also removes anything that may have gotten into the soil (the mind during the week that could hinder), preparing it to receive the seed.

What are we allowing that keeps us from worshipping (preparing) our soil for the promised benefits and harvest in the scriptures? We will look into and reveal the answer in the rest of this chapter.

Matthew 13:15

15 For the **hearts of these people are hardened**, and their ears cannot hear, and they have closed their eyes- so their eyes cannot see, and their ears cannot hear, and their hearts cannot understand, and they cannot turn to me and let me heal them. (NLT)

Mark 6:52

52 For they considered not *the miracle* of the loaves: **for their heart was hardened**.

Mark 16:14

14 Afterward he appeared unto the eleven as they sat at meat, and upbraided them with **their unbelief and hardness of heart**, because they believed not them which had seen him after he was risen.

Remember, a hard heart is often the result of unbelief, which is a decision, a choice, after you have heard or seen, then rejected it.

Romans 8:7 (DHP also)

Jeremiah, the prophet penned these very strong words:

Jeremiah 17:9

9 The heart *is* deceitful above all *things,* and desperately wicked: who can know it?

Some of the better definitions of the Hebrew word **heart** (from Strong's and Brown-Driver-Biggs) refers to the mind, will, and soul, the seat of man's appetites. The derivative of the Hebrew word #H6117 describes someone being tripped up around their heels. I know you are not necessarily supposed to do this when writing a book (but since it is mine…lol), WOW!!! When our mind and will are operating out of deception, we are the cause of being tripped up, the falls, and mistakes.

I feel this so strongly as I am writing the final thoughts of this chapter, I want to pray this prayer for myself and all those who will pray it with me (out loud) as you read it and it quickens something inside of us, even convicting us.

————

Father, we come to you in a true heart of repentance, forgive us for allowing the cares of this world and life to override the very principles you have spoken to us through your word. Today, right now, we choose, we purpose to once again become a people that understands your purpose for creating (forming) us was for your glory, and for your praise (**Isaiah 43:7,21**). This is the day that the true worshippers are rising up and fulfilling **John 4:23**, we desire to be those who worship you from the heart, in the right spirit and truth. No longer will we allow distractions, old mindsets, feelings, or emotions to steal our praise, our soil will be rich and prepared through our worship to receive your incorruptible seed (your kingdom message from your kingdom messenger). Our fruit will no longer be hindered, prolonged, or stopped because our heart, soil, and mind are right, then, coupled together with our praise, we will receive the 100-fold return as you declared in your Kingdom parable in **Matthew 13**. In the powerful, matchless name of Jesus, the Christ, Amen, and Amen.

---

1. John Gill, *Exposition of the Entire Bible* (published 1748-1763, 1809), accessed from e-Sword Online Bible, public domain.

IX) THE STONY GROUND
LESSON 9

Matthew 13:5,6, 20,21(DHP also)

Other meanings of the words, "stony places" are shallow, immature, carnal. I believe this type of soil also represents those who walk in and are easily offended. The sad part is, often many are swift to look at and judge others so quickly, but never truly look within to see the things that cause offense within themselves. Here is a verse that all of us should strive to develop and walk in:

Psalm 119:165

165 Great peace have they which love thy law: and nothing shall offend them.

165 Those who truly love God's instruction and teachings, nothing will steal their peace, cause a stumbling block or fall into offense. (DHP)

The Apostle Peter confirms these thoughts in his writings:

1 Peter 2:6-8

Peter affirms that Christ is the "chief corner stone" which is the first stone (rock) that is placed once the foundation is laid by the Apostles and Prophets (**See Ephesians 2:20**). Those who are disobedient to the revelation, those who reject the truths he taught cause their own stumbling which they then become offended at by rejecting them. I call it self-deception.

Earlier in Peter's life, he is the one that received and the first to declare that Jesus was the Christ. Once he proclaimed it, Jesus said to him, "…upon this rock I will build my church…" (**See Mathew 16:18-19**) Christ is the Chief Cornerstone (the rock), the message of Christ and the Kingdom (which was the message he preached) and that is a key given to Peter and now us to continue his message.

Often in those with this type of soil, there is a quick response, but because of the shallowness of the soil, it does not grow a deep root base. Charles Spurgeon once said, "Some folks seen to have been baptized in boiling water, requiring constant superficial excitement to remain in the faith. When trouble and persecution come, they leave quickly. Their idea of discipleship has no place for suffering, they are fair-weather Christians."

My guess is these types of individuals have never heard or were taught **1 Peter 5:10**:

10 But the God of all grace, who hath called us unto his eternal glory by Christ Jesus, after that ye have suffered a while, make you perfect, stablish, strengthen, settle you. (KJV)

10 After you have suffered for a little while, the God of all grace [who imparts His blessing and favor], who called you to His *own* eternal glory in Christ, will Himself complete, confirm, strengthen, and establish you [making you what you ought to be]. (The Amplified Bible)

10 And then, after your brief suffering, the God of all loving grace, who has called you to share in his eternal glory in Christ, will personally and powerfully restore you and make you stronger than ever. Yes, he will set you firmly in place and build you up. (TPT)

> **10** God who is rich in grace, loving kindness, and mercy has summoned us to participate in all that his glory reveals which is perpetual, eternal, forever, which has no end, which is ours through Christ as he is "**in us**" and we are "**in him**." You will experience some affliction, difficulties, distress and hardship for a little while (short seasons), these things are not meant to destroy or punish you, but to strengthen you and your beliefs, to equip you, to prepare you to walk in all that I have called you to, you will be become immoveable, strong with spiritual power and knowledge, all because your foundation is firm, solid, and cannot be shaken. (DHP)

Endurance is seldom taught let alone acted upon. However, there are promises to those who endure. **Matthew 24:13-14 (DHP also)** says:

The Jews referred to these stony places as barren, a place not fit for sowing. John Gill's notes in his commentary of **Verse 5** are a little lengthy however well worth the read so I added them here.

"And forthwith they sprung up, because they had no deepness of earth"; to strike their roots downwards: and through the reflection of the heat, upon the rocks and stones, they quickly broke through the thin surface of the earth over them, and appeared above ground before the usual time of the springing up of seed: which may not only denote the immediate reception of the word by these hearers, and their quick assent to it; but their sudden and hasty profession of it, without taking due time to consider the nature and importance thereof; and the seeming cheerfulness in which they did both receive and profess it; though it was only outward and hypocritical, and more on account of the manner of preaching it, than the word itself, and through a selfish principle in them; and did not arise from any real experience of the power of it on their souls, or true spiritual pleasure in it: nor could it be otherwise, since their stony hearts were not taken away, nor hearts of flesh given them; wherefore the word had no place in them, and made no real impression on them; they remained dead in trespasses and sins; the word was not the savour of life unto life unto them, or the Spirit that giveth life; they did not become living and lively stones; they continued as insensible as ever of their state and condition by nature, of the exceeding sinfulness of sin, of the danger they were in, and of their need of Christ, and salvation by him; they were as hard, and obdurate, and as inflexible, as ever, without any real contrition for sin, or meltings of soul through the influence of the love and grace of God; and as backward as ever to submit to the righteousness of Christ, being stout hearted, and far from it; and being no more cordially willing to be subject to the sceptre of his kingdom, or to serve him in righteousness and holiness, than they ever were; for the word falling upon them, made no change in them; their hearts were as hard as ever, notwithstanding the seeming and hasty reception of it; though they did not refuse to hearken to the word externally, did not put away the shoulder, or stop their ears, yet their hearts were still like an adamant stone: nothing but the mighty power of God, and his efficacious grace, can break the rocky heart in pieces; or give an heart of flesh, a sensible, soft, and flexible one, with which a man truly repents of sin, believes in Christ, and becomes subject to him.

Matthew 13:6,20,21 (DHP also)

Albert Barnes wrote, **"But he that received the seed into stony places."** - Jesus explains this as denoting those who hear the gospel; who are caught with it as something new or pleasing; who profess to be greatly delighted with it, and who are full of zeal for it.

Yet they have no root in themselves. They are not true Christians. Their hearts are not changed. They have not seen their guilt and danger, and the true excellency of Christ. They are not "really" attached to the gospel; and when they are tried and persecution comes, they fall - as the rootless grain withers before the scorching rays of the noonday sun. (Albert Barnes Commentary)

21 Yet hath he not root in himself, but dureth for a while: for when tribulation or persecution ariseth because of the word, by and by he is offended.

21 Shortly after he hears it, troubles and persecutions come because of the kingdom message he received. Then he quickly falls away, for the truth did not sink deeply into his heart. (**TPT**)

The Passion Translation states that this individual heard the "kingdom message" but almost immediately trouble and persecution came. Why? Not because of the person, but the potential the seed (message) carried. Why does he turn away? I believe he turned away having no insight, revelation, or illumination as to why the trouble and persecution came. Him taking **offense** (see **Verse 21** in the KJV above) so quickly in his soil (mind) stopped the seed's process, not allowing it into the innermost parts of his being.

The New American Standard Version says, "he has no firm root in himself."

The Amplified says, "he has no substantial root in himself."

Here is another thought to consider, he was never truly rooted and grounded in the "In Christ" realities to begin with. It may look like his soil (soul, mind) is deep, prepared, even fertile, but the rock, the hardness of heart, the offense, all the things to hinder the seed lay right under the shallow soil.

The phrase "hath not root in himself" really describes someone who has no depth of the seed (the Word of God) in them, possibly just enough to look the part, but not any depth to sustain him or his beliefs and actions when the persecution and trouble come.

> **21** The seed never fully develops as the soil is so shallow that the roots can't grow deep, thus his endurance is limited, minimal, and weak, so, when the pressure increases, when trouble and persecution come because of what the seed (message) is carrying and can manifest,

immediately his immaturity is exposed because he has no real confidence and trust in God, now he is offended at the messenger and the message and is tripped up and stumbles (falls). (DHP)

This type of individual is typical of many that believe in and profess Jesus to be their savior, but have yet to experience Him as Lord. They entered the door (which is Christ), but have remained in the outer court, only hearing a sin-conscious message, yet because of the type of church they attend, what their doctrines and beliefs are, and the message they have sat under, have never come into the revelation that there were three rooms in the Tabernacle of Moses, which was a type and shadow of what was to come, the Tabernacle of Jesus. They have not been taught that Jesus lives in a three-room house, you come in the outer court at the New Birth, then you move in Pentecost, the Holy Place and finally sonship, a mature son, the Holy of Holies where all the attributes of God are made manifest through His many-membered Christ (the mature sons) in the earth.

———

A few final thoughts as we close out this chapter. Excitement, shouting, running around the building, or even falling out in the presence of God is not the proof that the seed took, as all of us know and can relate who have lived a while on this earth. It has everything to do with the soil, the heart, and the mind. Selah!

The Stony ground because of the shallowness of its soil, with more rocks under the surface than the soil that can be seen on the surface speaks of never really being fully connected or fastened to the message of the kingdom. Even though the seed (message) was preached (sown), the seed never rooted, so the heat of the persecution singed the seed, stopped its growth, and no plant or fruit was produced.

X) THE THORNY GROUND
LESSON 10

Matthew 13:7,22 (DHP also)

Because the thorns still remained, the freshly sown seed was negatively impacted as the thorns choked the seeds potential.

"They grew with the grain, crowded it, shaded it, exhausted the earth, and thus choked it." (Albert Barnes Commentary)

The word deceitful can also represent the way in which the wrong desire to be rich deceives people. These deceptions will steal their time and attention which instead should be placed on the condition of their own soil (mind), the reason for their inability to manifest the fruit hidden in the seed (message).

They have never learned, let alone applied the truths in **1 Peter 5:7**:

7 Casting all your care upon him; for he careth for you.

7 Casting all your cares [all your anxieties, all your worries, and all your concerns, once and for all] on Him, for He cares about you [with deepest affection, and watches over you very carefully]. (Amplified Bible)

> **7** Throw the entirety, every anxious distraction, anything that would disunite (affect your unity) with him and his word, take your rest in him, He takes great interest in you and he cares about the things you have need of. (DHP)

King David (the psalmist) echoes the same sentiment as the Apostle Peter penned:

Psalm 55:22

22 Cast thy burden upon the LORD, and he shall sustain thee: he shall never suffer the righteous to be moved.

Cast every care, burden, trial, persecution, and affliction upon the Lord. Why? He will hold you up, he will sustain you as go through it. However, this promise is to the righteous. Yes, his death, burial, and resurrection over sin, sickness and the grave gave us his righteousness (see **2 Corinthians 5:21**), however, we still must walk in and operate through our right standing with him.

The word **righteous** in **Verse 22** is the Hebrew word, *"tsaddîyq"* (pronounced: tsad-deek') and translates as, "right/righteous in government, cause, conduct, character, correct and lawful. As you well know, there are those who Christ has made his righteousness available to but at present are not demonstrating/walking in it. The promise of not "being moved" belongs to them. The Hebrew word for **moved** is *"môṭ"* (pronounced: mote') and describes someone who cannot be, "shaken, overthrown or dislodged."

The Apostle Paul in writing to the church in Philippi exhorted with the same thoughts when he wrote his letter to them:

Philippians 4:6-7

The word **careful** is the Greek word, "*merimnaō*" (pronounced: mer-im-nah'-o) which speaks of not becoming anxious (side note: many today are on strong anxiety drugs that only numb them and mask the true issue and can lead to serious mental and physical issues), becoming completely occupied with the wrong thoughts.

Adam Clarke said in his commentary, anxiety cannot change the state or condition of anything from bad to good, but will infallibly injure your own souls. If we will learn and implement this truth, look at the promises in **Verse 7.**

Releasing the cares of this life will keep us in peace, it will keep your heart and mind as we learn to operate in the Mind of Christ (see **1 Corinthians 2:16**) which we now have access to.

The word **keep** is powerful in the Greek language, it is the word, "*phroureō*" (pronounced: froo-reh'-o) and defines as, "to guard, to protect by a military guard, to prevent a hostile invasion, to place a guard as a sentinel (a soldier/guard whose job is to stand and keep watch).

The Thorny ground (soil) will quickly respond at first, then they are overcome with worries, greed, worldly desires (as they have not yet died to their flesh), offense, wrong choices, and decisions which all will choke the seed (word), effecting their spiritual life to the point no spiritual fruit is developed.

Notice our text passage again that began this chapter, **Verse 7**, the seed was sown, the message was preached, but that soil was full of thorns which overtook the seed.

Being consumed with cares and worries steals all their time and demands their attention so they have no time to honestly look at the condition of their own soil. This type of soil is never satisfied because it always demands more, enough is never enough. The temptation becomes overwhelming to being dishonest, to cheat, to do whatever it takes to get more, even using and taking advantage of others. Money in/of itself is not evil, how one gets it, that is another story. The Bible reminds us:

1 Timothy 6:10

The riches/cares of this world entice with an ungodly allurement which will always promise something it cannot and will not deliver. Some speak of the happiness/joy that money brings, but when gained, especially the world's way, it brings sorrow. Herein lies the difference, God's way versus the world's way.

Albert Barnes penned these powerful thoughts in his commentary, *"How many, O how many, thus foolishly drown themselves in destruction and perdition! How many more might reach heaven, if it were not for this deep-seated love of that which fills the mind with care, deceives the soul, and finally leaves it naked, and guilty, and lost!"*

There is a right way, a kingdom way to receive God's abundance, yet it must be done His way through His word. This may take more time in the natural, you have seed…time…then…harvest.

You have to receive the seed, let it become planted, water the seed, sun the seed, weed around the seed, and as the root system becomes established deep in the soil, the fruit springs up, matures, then harvested.

Proverbs 10:22 (DHP also)

The thorny soil describes the unproductive/fruitless lives of individuals who allow the cares of life to take precedence in their mind, consuming their thoughts instead of taking those thoughts captive. Then, the thorns suffocate the seeds' potential that they heard, and no fruit ever develops. Discouragement sets in, the blame game starts, pointing fingers at everyone and everything, never thinking they might need to look inward, into their own soil (mind) as to the hindrance.

Do we still not discern or understand starting in Genesis (the book of beginnings) and on, soil played a very key, important role throughout the scriptures? We came from dirt, our first parents, Adam and Eve were gardeners, responsible to cultivate (farm, develop, and plow) the very ground they/we came from. Then, the amazing thing is Jesus's stories of agriculture, farming, seed, soil, and harvest describing/explaining the kingdom.

———

As we close out this chapter, I pray for you, the reader and myself.

"Lord let the scales be removed from our eyes. We give Holy Spirit permission to take us deep into the hidden recesses of our soil, mind, and heart. Convict us of operating in any soil but that which You call good. Show us, then we will act, respond, acknowledge, and change our heart condition. We know that You do not condemn, You convict for our good. Today will begin a new day, a new soil will emerge, and a different outcome is eminent.

The fruit that comes will be mature, fully developed because of the right soil, and it will remain. It will not rot, or come to ruin. It will be a blessing in our lives as well as all that we encounter on this journey. In the name of Jesus, we call it done, and give You all the praise and glory for finishing the work in/through us that You began.

The fruit that is coming will bring glory to Your name. The past is forgiven, forgotten, removed and is no longer a hindrance to my purpose, calling and destiny. Amen and amen!

XI) THE GOOD GROUND (SOIL)

LESSON 11

Matthew 13:8,23 (Also DHP)

An interesting thought here: In this kingdom parable, Jesus stated the good (best) soil receiving this message (seed) had the potential of 100-fold, then He stated others in the "same soil" only experienced 60-fold, and some only 30-fold. God is not a respecter of persons, but He is of principles. He does not value one more important than another. So, the person receiving 100-fold, 60-fold, or 30-fold in good ground would lend itself to believe that the individual determines what measure of the message they are going to receive.

Do they hear, then settle for a 60-fold or 30-fold return (harvest)? Do our thoughts, words, and actions on the message sown into our soil set boundaries hindering the seed's full potential? Do we settle for 60 because we have never experienced what it is like to enjoy the 100, or 30 in view of never experiencing the 60? Our words can stunt the seeds' potential, or release the seeds' fullest potential.

In Biblical numerics, the number 100 speaks of being children of promise. Why settle for anything less than the best He has promised? Also notice in this kingdom parable, Jesus starts with 100, then goes down from there. Often, I hear ministers reference this as 30, 60, and 100-fold, however, in this parable, Jesus reveals the seed's capacity beginning with the best, 100-fold.

———

While looking at these two verses something grabbed my attention that I had missed in the research, study, and writing of this new manuscript. So I went back and reread the usage of the certain words, uncovering something I had missed.

Matthew 13:4,5,7,8

Verse 4 "some seeds fell **by (Greek-beside, near)** the wayside…"

Verse 5 "Some fell **upon (Greek-against, towards)** stony places…"

Verse 7 "And some fell **among (Greek-same words as upon)** thorns…"

Verse 8 "But other fell **into (Greek-in the presence of, immediately upon, came to rest in/on)** good ground…"

The seed was the same in this kingdom parable, the word of God (seed) is called incorruptible (it cannot decay, come to ruin, it is imperishable). The Sower scattered (sowed) the seed but it fell among four different soils (if you will, four different types of people). The first seed fell "**by**" the wayside, the second fell "**upon**" the stony places, the third fell "**among**" the thorns, and the fourth fell "**into**" good ground.

Notice the meaning of the four soils from the Greek listed above. Seed **beside or near** will not work, seed **against or towards** will not produce, seed **among (against, towards)** will not completely develop, but the seed that comes **into the presence of**, that **comes into and rests in/on** the good soil comes to maturity.

The good soil represents disciples in the truest sense of the word; they are students, pupils, listeners, and learners. They understand the process, and at times, the suffering they will go through for a season. They understand that purging/pruning seasons are not punishment, but preparation.

When was the last time we honestly assessed our own discipleship? How do we hear, yet even more important, receive and act on God's Word? Our reception of this kingdom message and the fruit that should follow is determined by the condition of our soil (heart, soul). It is not based on the messenger (five-fold, ascension giftings).

Have we prepared our hearts to receive it, then allow the process of the seed to work in/under the soil (the unseen realm), giving it the time needed to bring externally the DNA that resides in the seed internally?

Let us look at two of the gospels that both reference the **good** versus evil **heart**.

Matthew 12:33-35 (Also DHP)

Another thought of interest to reflect on concerning the wording of **Verse 33** in the KJV. Jesus refers to the good tree as, "**his**," the corrupt tree as, "**his**," and the fruit of both as, "**his**" three times is this verse, calling the tree a gender. I believe the prophetic implication here is referencing the tree as people and what type of fruit they produce.

This might be a stretch for some, but look at this passage in light of the above comment:

Mark 8:22-25

22 And he cometh to Bethsaida; and they bring a blind man unto him, and besought him to touch him.

23 And he took the blind man by the hand, and led him out of the town; and when he had spit on his eyes, and put his hands upon him, he asked him if he saw ought.

24 And he looked up, and said, **I see men as trees, walking**.

25 After that he put *his* hands again upon his eyes, and made him look up: and he was restored, and saw every man clearly.

Interestingly enough, during his healing process he sees men as trees.

The works will resemble the heart: nothing good can proceed from an evil spirit; no good fruit can proceed from a corrupt heart. Before the heart of man can produce any good, it must be renewed and influenced by the Spirit of God. (Adam Clarke Commentary)

The tree is not known because of its leaves, its form, width, height, or its bark (the outer covering), it is known by the fruit it produces. The DNA (blueprint) of a tree is designed to grow, develop, mature, and manifest the fruit **externally** of what already exists **internally**.

Matthew 12:34-35 (Also DHP)

Luke 6:43-45

43 For a good tree bringeth not forth corrupt fruit; neither doth a corrupt tree bring forth good fruit.

> **43** A tree that is genuine, useful, honorable, and noble does not bring forth rotten fruit, unfit for use, nor does a corrupt (impure) tree bear/produce valuable precious fruit. (DHP)

44 For every tree is known by his own fruit. For of thorns men do not gather figs, nor of a bramble bush gather they grapes.

> **44** Every tree produces from what it is intimate with, what it is intimate with privately will be seen publicly. Thorns and briars cannot harvest figs, neither can shrubs full of thorns harvest grapes. (DHP)

Good and Bad Fruit.—Christ here speaks of the inner nature— the heart—of man and of its outward manifestations, and asserts that in all cases the inner is the maker of the outward. A good heart will infallibly reveal itself in holiness of word and deed: in like manner an evil heart will disclose itself, in spite of all hypocritical attempts to conceal the true state of matters. (Preachers Homiletical Commentary)

The Greek word for **tree** in **Verse 44** is, *"hekastos"* (pronounced: hek'-as-tos) which also defines as, "every man and woman."

45 A good man out of the good treasure of his heart bringeth forth that which is good; and an evil man out of the evil treasure of his heart bringeth forth that which is evil: for of the abundance of the heart his mouth speaketh.

> **45** The good man who is upright and virtuous brings forth and produces what is profitable, that good which he has stored up in his mind will be made manifest and seen for the excellent qualities it possesses. The evil man whose nature, character, and motives are unethical can/will only reveal the DNA of those wicked, unsound, flaws in his storehouse because his mind has never been renewed. The good man and evil man will both make known what is hidden in their heart as that which fills the heart (mind), their lips will give voice to what the mind is filled with. (DHP)

The word **heart** is the Greek word, *"kardia"* (pronounced: kar-dee'-ah) which also refers to the, "thoughts or feelings of the mind, of the soul so far as it is affected and stirred in a bad way or good, or of the soul as the seat of the sensibilities, affections, emotions, desires, appetites, passions."

The word **mouth** in Thayer's G4750 is the Greek word, *"stoma"* (pronounced: stom'-a), it states, "since thoughts of a man's soul find verbal utterance by his mouth, the "heart" or "soul" and the mouth are distinguished."

At this point in writing this chapter, I was once again reminded of a portion of scripture that will further our understanding of fruit.

James 5:7-8 (Also DHP)

In the natural, Israel is known to have two main rainfalls a year. The early rain (former) which happens in October, and the latter rain which falls in March and April just before the harvest. (Also see **Joel 2:23.**)

Let me add to the foundation being laid in this chapter, let's re-look at **John 15:1-8** (italics added for emphasis):

1 I am the true vine, and **my Father is the husbandman.**

2 Every branch in me that beareth not fruit he taketh away: and **every *branch* that beareth fruit, he purgeth it, that it may bring forth more fruit.**

3 Now **ye are clean through the word** which I have spoken unto you.

4 Abide in me, and I in you. As **the branch cannot bear fruit of itself, except it abide in the vine**; no more can ye, except ye abide in me.

5 I am the vine, ye *are* the branches: He that abideth in me, and I in him, the same bringeth forth much fruit: for without me ye can do nothing.

6 If a man abide not in me, he is cast forth as a branch, and is withered; and men gather them, and cast *them* into the fire, and they are burned.

7 If ye abide in me, and my words abide in you, ye shall ask what ye will, and it shall be done unto you.

8 Herein is my Father glorified, that ye bear much fruit; so shall ye be my disciples.

In the Apostle John's letter in the gospels, he speaks to the Godhead's function and responsibilities as well as the branches. God as the farmer planted, He planted in Eden, He planted His son as a seed into the earth which is the vine (**Galatians 3:16**), then redemption put that seed (Christ) in us. Now, we have become the branches which the vine produces.

Verse 2 expresses the purpose/process of purging, it is not a disciplinarian action but a preparation (preparing) us for the next season of manifesting more fruit. **More** is the Greek word, "*pleion*" (pronounced: pli-own) which defines as, "more in quality, quantity, more excellent, superior."

To produce fruit, the branches (us) must **abide** (Greek word, "*meno*" which means to, "remain, to stay in the presence of, to dwell") IN HIM (the vine). This does not happen in one hour of corporate worship and word on Sunday! It is a lifestyle, it is a student, disciple, a studier (not just a reader) of God's Word. The promise for the abiding branch is "much fruit" (**Verse 5**).

Verse 8 shares the Father's heart, He is glorified when His children produce, bear, and reveal fruit. He ends the verse with the phrase, "so shall you be my disciples." The reference here is what true discipleship looks like, they have stayed planted in the good soil, they have passed the tests and trials that came their way, their character remained intact (not damaged or impaired), fruit is the trophy if you will of faithful discipleship.

———

Consider this:

The Father God is the farmer (Husbandman).

Jesus is the True Vine.

The Holy Spirit is the life source (the sap that circulates in the vascular system of the plant) which flows from the vine (Jesus). He is the oil.

The Ekklesia (the true church, the many-membered body of Christ) is the branches of the vine where ultimately the fruit comes through.

The good soil has not been beaten or trodden by the feet of men, there are no stones or thorns in it. It has been well plowed, tilled, and fertilized which describes honest- hearted hearers who are led by the Spirit, those who have spiritual understanding because of their prayer and study time.

They have not just heard these truths, they have lived them out through life's struggles and attacks, they understand the process and are all the better for it. Their life, choices, and actions have allowed the seed to remain from the planting (sowing) process till it is matured and ready for harvest. Their soil (mind, heart) is rich, clutter free, and revealing the 100-fold return as promised by the Lord in this parable.

They have totally submitted themselves to the Truth, refusing to allow the cares and anxieties of this life to overtake the seeds' potential. The seeds' root system runs deep as there is nothing in their soil to hinder its full production. And finally, the seed's harvest leaves no room to doubt their soil condition.

ABOUT THE AUTHOR

Dr. Don Hughes is a seasoned, processed Apostolic voice with four plus (4+) decades of ministry throughout the U.S. and abroad. He has ministered in Africa, the Philippines, Korea, Mexico, and Canada as well as pioneered and raised up Churches in the United States.

Dr. Hughes leads and gives oversight to REV House Fellowship (a home ministry based on discipleship, relationship, and fellowship with an added emphasis on helping establish people in their gifting and function).

He is on the Senior Council of Love & Unity Fellowship based out of California, which is a nation-wide group of ministry leaders, men, and women, made up of all cultures, encouraging, fellowshipping, and challenging each other to stay the course.

He is the founder and lead instructor of REV House School of Ministry, which is a 2-year online school preparing, and training ministers, leaders, and laity.

He gives Apostolic leadership to Churches, leaders, spiritual sons, and daughters throughout the U.S. He is a 3rd generation minister and is the son of Dr. Don Hughes, Sr. (enjoying his eternal reward) who was a well-known author and requested speaker throughout much of the Word of Faith Movement.

He is an avid student and studier of God's Word and loves to research using the Hebrew and Greek to reveal truth that is all too often missed by simply reading the scriptures. Dr. Hughes will challenge, encourage, and bless you with his school of ministry, books, paraphrase/commentaries, word studies, conferences, and apostolic leadership equipping and training.

Dr. Hughes lives in East Oklahoma with his wife Lisa.

ALSO BY DR. DON D. HUGHES

The Book of Revelation: The Unveiling of Jesus Christ

The Prophecy, The Process, The Promise

Available on Amazon.com

The following titles and other merchandise is available on the RHSOM website www.rhsom.com/services-4 (under the PRODUCTS tab)

Money Myths, Misunderstandings & Mindsets: Revealed From A Biblical Perspective

Stones Aren't For Throwing

The 3rd Day (The Spirit of Revelation)

Will The Spiritual Ones Please Come Forward?

Contact Dr. Don Hughes at www.RHSOM.com or email at RHSOM. School@outlook.com

Made in the USA
Columbia, SC
30 November 2024

47823723R00141